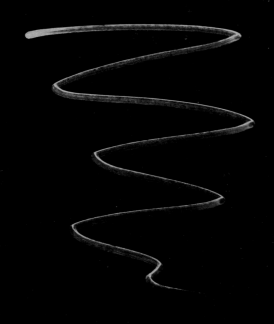

D1213223

THE PASTOR'S IDEAL
FUNERAL MANUAL

Edited by

NOLAN B. HARMON

Comfort ye, comfort ye my people, saith your God.
—Isa. 40:1

ABINGDON PRESS

New York • *Nashville*

THE PASTOR'S IDEAL FUNERAL MANUAL

Copyright MCMXLII by Whitmore & Stone

Library of Congress Catalog Card Number: 43-4032

SECOND EDITION

I

SET UP, PRINTED, AND BOUND BY THE
PARTHENON PRESS, AT NASHVILLE,
TENNESSEE, UNITED STATES OF AMERICA

HOW TO USE THIS MANUAL

This book is designed to help you, the pastor, in your funeral ministry. To use it to the best advantage, you should familiarize yourself with it in advance.

If you wish to use one of the standard liturgies in Part I, study the alternatives offered in the rubrics and note which will meet your needs. If you prefer to construct your own service, follow the suggestions in the Appendix, "The Service in Detail," or compose your own order. The scripture readings, prayers, and committals in the liturgies, together with those in Part II and the hymns and poems in Part III, will supply appropriate materials under each heading in your outline. The Index by Classifications at the end of the book will help you quickly find what you need.

Primarily the book is for use in the service itself. To this end it has been designed to be appropriate in appearance and easily readable whether held in the hand or lying on pulpit or lectern. The reading of all but original words from a single book adds to the impressiveness of the service. A further hint—if you use slips of paper as bookmarks, insert them, numbered in proper order on a lower corner, to project only about a quarter inch from the *bottom* of the book; thus they will be practically unnoticed by your hearers.

You will find in this Manual material which countless numbers of pastors today and through the years have found effective for the funeral. It is presented in the hope that its collection and arrangement in this volume will make easier a difficult and most important pastoral duty and privilege.

N. B. H., Jr.

CONTENTS

Part I
FUNERAL LITURGIES

THE PROTESTANT EPISCOPAL
SERVICE

From *The Book of Common Prayer*

*The Minister, meeting the Body, and going before it,
either into the Church or towards the Grave, shall
say or sing,*

I AM the resurrection and the life, saith the
Lord: he that believeth in me, though he
were dead, yet shall he live: and whosoever
liveth and believeth in me, shall never die.

I know that my redeemer liveth, and that
he shall stand at the latter day upon the earth:
and though this body be destroyed, yet shall I
see God: whom I shall see for myself, and
mine eyes shall behold, and not as a stranger.

We brought nothing into this world, and it
is certain we can carry nothing out. The Lord
gave, and the Lord hath taken away; blessed
be the name of the LORD.

*After they are come into the Church, shall be said
one or more of the following Selections, taken from
the Psalms. The Gloria Patri may be omitted except at the end of the whole portion or selection
from the Psalter.*

Dixi, custodiam. Psalm 39

LORD, let me know mine end, and the number of my days; that I may be certified how long I have to live.

Behold, thou hast made my days as it were a span long, and mine age is even as nothing in respect of thee; and verily every man living is altogether vanity.

For man walketh in a vain shadow, and disquieteth himself in vain; he heapeth up riches, and cannot tell who shall gather them.

And now, Lord, what is my hope? truly my hope is even in thee.

Deliver me from all mine offences; and make me not a rebuke unto the foolish.

When thou with rebukes dost chasten man for sin, thou makest his beauty to consume away, like as it were a moth fretting a garment: every man therefore is but vanity.

Hear my prayer, O Lord, and with thine ears consider my calling; hold not thy peace at my tears;

For I am a stranger with thee, and a sojourner, as all my fathers were.

O spare me a little, that I may recover my strength, before I go hence, and be no more seen.

Domine, refugium.   Psalm 90

LORD, thou hast been our refuge, from one generation to another.

Before the mountains were brought forth, or ever the earth and the world were made, thou art God from everlasting, and world without end.

Thou turnest man to destruction; again thou sayest, Come again, ye children of men.

For a thousand years in thy sight are but as yesterday, when it is past, and as a watch in the night.

As soon as thou scatterest them they are even as a sleep; and fade away suddenly like the grass.

In the morning it is green, and groweth up; but in the evening it is cut down, dried up, and withered.

For we consume away in thy displeasure, and are afraid at thy wrathful indignation.

Thou hast set our misdeeds before thee; and our secret sins in the light of thy countenance.

For when thou art angry all our days are gone: we bring our years to an end, as it were a tale that is told.

The days of our age are threescore years and ten; and though men be so strong that they come to fourscore years, yet is their strength then but labour and sorrow; so soon passeth it away, and we are gone.

So teach us to number our days, that we may apply our hearts unto wisdom.

Dominus illuminatio. Psalm 27

THE Lord is my light and my salvation; whom then shall I fear? the Lord is the strength of my life; of whom then shall I be afraid?

One thing have I desired of the Lord, which I will require; even that I may dwell in the house of the Lord all the days of my life, to behold the fair beauty of the Lord, and to visit his temple.

For in the time of trouble he shall hide me in his tabernacle; yea, in the secret place of his dwelling shall he hide me, and set me up upon a rock of stone.

And now shall he lift up mine head above mine enemies round about me.

Therefore will I offer in his dwelling an oblation, with great gladness: I will sing and speak praises unto the Lord.

Hearken unto my voice, O Lord, when I cry unto thee; have mercy upon me, and hear me.

My heart hath talked of thee, Seek ye my face: Thy face, Lord, will I seek.

O hide not thou thy face from me, nor cast thy servant away in displeasure.

Thou hast been my succour; leave me not, neither forsake me, O God of my salvation.

I should utterly have fainted, but that I believe verily to see the goodness of the Lord in the land of the living.

O tarry thou the Lord's leisure; be strong, and he shall comfort thine heart; and put thou thy trust in the Lord.

Deus noster refugium.   Psalm 46

God is our hope and strength, a very present help in trouble.

Therefore will we not fear, though the earth be moved, and though the hills be carried into the midst of the sea;

Though the waters thereof rage and swell, and though the mountains shake at the tempest of the same.

There is a river, the streams whereof make glad the city of God; the holy place of the tabernacle of the Most Highest.

God is in the midst of her, therefore shall

she not be removed; God shall help her, and that right early.

Be still then, and know that I am God: I will be exalted among the nations, and I will be exalted in the earth.

The Lord of hosts is with us; the God of Jacob is our refuge.

Levavi oculos. Psalm 121

I WILL lift up mine eyes unto the hills; from whence cometh my help?

My help cometh even from the Lord, who hath made heaven and earth.

He will not suffer thy foot to be moved; and he that keepeth thee will not sleep.

Behold, he that keepeth Israel shall neither slumber nor sleep.

The Lord himself is thy keeper; the Lord is thy defence upon thy right hand;

So that the sun shall not burn thee by day, neither the moon by night.

The Lord shall preserve thee from all evil; yea, it is even he that shall keep thy soul.

The Lord shall preserve thy going out, and thy coming in, from this time forth for evermore.

De profundis. Psalm 130

OUT of the deep have I called unto thee, O Lord; Lord, hear my voice.

O let thine ears consider well the voice of my complaint.

If thou, Lord, wilt be extreme to mark what is done amiss, O Lord, who may abide it?

For there is mercy with thee; therefore shalt thou be feared.

I look for the Lord; my soul doth wait for him; in his word is my trust.

My soul fleeth unto the Lord before the morning watch; I say, before the morning watch.

O Israel, trust in the Lord, for with the Lord there is mercy, and with him is plenteous redemption.

And he shall redeem Israel from all his sins.

Then shall follow the Lesson, taken out of the fifteenth Chapter of the first Epistle of St. Paul to the Corinthians.

1 Corinthians 15:20-58

NOW is Christ risen from the dead, and become the firstfruits of them that slept. For since by man came death, by man came also the resurrection of the dead. For as in

Adam all die, even so in Christ shall all be made alive. But every man in his own order: Christ the firstfruits; afterward they that are Christ's at his coming. Then cometh the end, when he shall have delivered up the kingdom to God, even the Father; when he shall have put down all rule and all authority and power. For he must reign, till he hath put all enemies under his feet. The last enemy that shall be destroyed is death. For he hath put all things under his feet. But when he saith all things are put under him, it is manifest that he is excepted, which did put all things under him. And when all things shall be subdued unto him, then shall the Son also himself be subject unto him that put all things under him, that God may be all in all.

But some man will say, How are the dead raised up? and with what body do they come? Thou foolish one, that which thou sowest is not quickened, except it die: and that which thou sowest, thou sowest not that body that shall be, but bare grain, it may chance of wheat, or of some other grain: but God giveth it a body as it hath pleased him, and to every seed its own body. All flesh is not the same flesh: but there is one kind of flesh of men, another flesh of beasts, another of fishes, and another of birds. There are also celestial bodies, and bodies terrestrial: but the glory of the celestial is one, and the glory of the terrestrial is another. There is one glory of the sun, and another glory of the moon, and another glory of the stars: for one star differeth from another star in glory. So also is the resurrection of the dead. It is sown in corruption; it is raised in incorruption: it is sown in dishonour; it is raised in glory: it is sown in weakness; it is raised in power: it is sown a natural body; it is raised a spiritual body. There is a natural body, and there is a spiritual body. And so it is written, The first man Adam was made a living soul; the last Adam was made a quickening spirit. Howbeit that was not first which is spiritual, but that which is natural; and afterward that which is spiritual. The first man is of the earth, earthy: the second man is the Lord from heaven. As is the earthy, such are they also that are earthy: and as is the heavenly, such are they also that are heavenly. And as we have borne the image of the earthy, we shall also bear the image of the heavenly.

Now this I say, brethren, that flesh and blood cannot inherit the kingdom of God;

neither doth corruption inherit incorruption. Behold, I shew you a mystery; We shall not all sleep, but we shall all be changed, in a moment, in the twinkling of an eye, at the last trump: for the trumpet shall sound, and the dead shall be raised incorruptible, and we shall be changed. For this corruptible must put on incorruption, and this mortal must put on immortality. So when this corruptible shall have put on incorruption, and this mortal shall have put on immortality, then shall be brought to pass the saying that is written, Death is swallowed up in victory. O death, where is thy sting? O grave, where is thy victory? The sting of death is sin; and the strength of sin is the law. But thanks be to God, which giveth us the victory through our Lord Jesus Christ. Therefore, my beloved brethren, be ye stedfast, unmoveable, always abounding in the work of the Lord, forasmuch as ye know that your labour is not in vain in the Lord.

Or this:
Romans 8:14-19, 28, 31, 32, 34, 35, 37-39

As many as are led by the Spirit of God, they are the sons of God. For ye have not received the spirit of bondage again to fear; but

ye have received the Spirit of adoption, whereby we cry, Abba, Father. The Spirit himself
beareth witness with our spirit, that we are the
children of God: and if children, then heirs;
heirs of God, and joint-heirs with Christ; if so
be that we suffer with him, that we may be also
glorified together. For I reckon that the sufferings of this present time are not worthy to
be compared with the glory which shall be revealed in us. For the earnest expectation of
the creature waiteth for the manifestation of
the sons of God. We know that all things
work together for good to them that love God,
to them who are the called according to his
purpose. What shall we then say to these
things? If God be for us, who can be against
us? He that spared not his own Son, but delivered him up for us all, how shall he not with
him also freely give us all things? Who is he
that condemneth? It is Christ that died, yea
rather, that is risen again, who is even at the
right hand of God, who also maketh intercession for us. Who shall separate us from the
love of Christ? shall tribulation, or distress, or
persecution, or famine, or nakedness, or peril,
or sword? Nay, in all these things we are more
than conquerors through him that loved us.

For I am persuaded, that neither death, nor life, nor angels, nor principalities, nor powers, nor things present, nor things to come, nor height, nor depth, nor any other creature, shall be able to separate us from the love of God, which is in Christ Jesus our Lord.

Or this:
St. John 14:1-6

JESUS said, Let not your heart be troubled: ye believe in God, believe also in me. In my Father's house are many mansions: if it were not so, I would have told you. I go to prepare a place for you. And if I go and prepare a place for you, I will come again, and receive you unto myself; that where I am, there ye may be also. And whither I go ye know, and the way ye know. Thomas saith unto him, Lord, we know not whither thou goest; and how can we know the way? Jesus saith unto him, I am the way, the truth, and the life: no man cometh unto the Father, but by me.

Here may be sung a Hymn or Anthem; and, at the discretion of the Minister, the Creed, the Lord's Prayer, the Prayer which followeth, and such other fitting Prayers as are elsewhere provided in this

*Book, ending with the Blessing; the Minister, be-
fore the Prayers, first pronouncing,*

The Lord be with you.
Answer.   And with thy spirit.

Let us pray.

REMEMBER thy servant, O Lord, according
to the favour which thou bearest unto thy
people, and grant that, increasing in knowledge
and love of thee, *he* may go from strength to
strength, in the life of perfect service, in thy
heavenly kingdom; through Jesus Christ our
Lord, who liveth and reigneth with thee and
the Holy Ghost ever, one God, world without
end. *Amen.*

UNTO God's gracious mercy and protection
we commit you. The Lord bless you
and keep you. The Lord make his face to
shine upon you, and be gracious unto you.
The Lord lift up his countenance upon you,
and give you peace, both now and evermore.
Amen.

AT THE GRAVE

When they come to the Grave, while the Body is made ready to be laid into the earth, shall be sung or said,

MAN, that is born of a woman, hath but a short time to live, and is full of misery. He cometh up, and is cut down, like a flower; he fleeth as it were a shadow, and never continueth in one stay.

In the midst of life we are in death; of whom may we seek for succour, but of thee, O Lord, who for our sins art justly displeased?

Yet, O Lord God most holy, O Lord most mighty, O holy and most merciful Saviour, deliver us not into the bitter pains of eternal death.

Thou knowest, Lord, the secrets of our hearts; shut not thy merciful ears to our prayer; but spare us, Lord most holy, O God most mighty, O holy and merciful Saviour, thou most worthy Judge eternal, suffer us not, at our last hour, for any pains of death, to fall from thee.

Or this

A LL that the Father giveth me shall come to me; and him that cometh to me I will in no wise cast out.

He that raised up Jesus from the dead will also quicken our mortal bodies, by his Spirit that dwelleth in us.

Wherefore my heart is glad, and my glory rejoiceth: my flesh also shall rest in hope.

Thou shalt show me the path of life; in thy presence is the fulness of joy, and at thy right hand there is pleasure for evermore.

Then, while the earth shall be cast upon the Body by some standing by, the Minister shall say,

U NTO Almighty God we commend the soul of our *brother* departed, and we commit *his* body to the ground; earth to earth, ashes to ashes, dust to dust; in sure and certain hope of the Resurrection unto eternal life, through our Lord Jesus Christ; at whose coming in glorious majesty to judge the world, the earth and the sea shall give up their dead; and the corruptible bodies of those who sleep in him shall be changed, and made like unto his own glorious body; according to the mighty working whereby he is able to subdue all things unto himself.

Then shall be said or sung,

I HEARD a voice from heaven, saying unto me, Write, From henceforth blessed are the dead who die in the Lord: even so saith the Spirit; for they rest from their labours.

Then the Minister shall say,

The Lord be with you.
Answer.   And with thy spirit.

Let us pray.

Lord, have mercy upon us.
Christ, have mercy upon us.
Lord, have mercy upon us.

OUR Father, who art in heaven, Hallowed be thy Name. Thy kingdom come. Thy will be done, On earth as it is in heaven. Give us this day our daily bread. And forgive us our trespasses, As we forgive those who trespass against us. And lead us not into temptation, But deliver us from evil. *Amen.*

Then the Minister shall say one or more of the following Prayers, at his discretion.

O GOD, whose mercies cannot be numbered; Accept our prayers on behalf of the soul of thy servant departed, and grant *him* an entrance into the land of light and joy, in the fellowship of thy saints; through Jesus Christ our Lord. *Amen.*

A LMIGHTY God, with whom do live the spirits of those who depart hence in the Lord, and with whom the souls of the faithful, after they are delivered from the burden of the flesh, are in joy and felicity; We give thee hearty thanks for the good examples of all those thy servants, who, having finished their course in faith, do now rest from their labours. And we beseech thee, that we, with all those who are departed in the true faith of thy holy Name, may have our perfect consummation and bliss, both in body and soul, in thy eternal and everlasting glory; through Jesus Christ our Lord. *Amen.*

O MERCIFUL God, the Father of our Lord Jesus Christ, who is the Resurrection and the Life; in whom whosoever believeth, shall live, though he die; and whosoever liveth, and believeth in him, shall not die eternally; who also hath taught us, by his holy Apostle Saint Paul, not to be sorry, as men without hope, for those who sleep in him; We humbly beseech thee, O Father, to raise us from the death of sin unto the life of righteousness; that, when we shall depart this life, we may rest in him; and that, at the general Resurrection in the last day, we may be found acceptable in thy sight; and receive that blessing, which thy well-beloved Son shall then pronounce to all who love and fear thee, saying, Come, ye blessed children of my Father, receive the kingdom prepared for you from the beginning of the world. Grant this, we beseech thee, O merciful Father, through Jesus Christ, our Mediator and Redeemer. *Amen.*

THE God of peace, who brought again from the dead our Lord Jesus Christ, the great Shepherd of the sheep, through the blood of the everlasting covenant; Make you perfect in every good work to do his will, working in you that which is well pleasing in his sight; through Jesus Christ, to whom be glory for ever and ever. *Amen.*

The Minister, at his discretion, may also use any of the following Prayers before the final Blessing.

O ALMIGHTY God, the God of the spirits of all flesh, who by a voice from heaven didst proclaim, Blessed are the dead who die in the Lord; Multiply, we beseech thee, to those who rest in Jesus, the manifold blessings of thy love, that the good work which thou didst begin in them may be perfected unto the day of Jesus Christ. And of thy mercy, O heavenly Father, vouchsafe that we, who now serve thee here on earth, may at last, together with them, be found meet to be partakers of the inheritance of the saints in light; for the sake of the same thy Son Jesus Christ our Lord. *Amen.*

MOST merciful Father, who hast been pleased to take unto thyself the soul of this thy servant (*or* this thy child); Grant to us who are still in our pilgrimage, and who walk as yet by faith, that having served thee with constancy on earth, we may be joined hereafter with thy blessed saints in glory everlasting; through Jesus Christ our Lord. *Amen.*

O LORD Jesus Christ, who by thy death didst take away the sting of death; Grant unto us thy servants so to follow in faith where thou hast led the way, that we may at length fall asleep peacefully in thee, and awake up after thy likeness; through thy mercy, who livest with the Father and the Holy Ghost, one God, world without end. *Amen.*

ALMIGHTY and everliving God, we yield unto thee most high praise and hearty thanks, for the wonderful grace and virtue declared in all thy saints, who have been the choice vessels of thy grace, and the lights of the world in their several generations; most humbly beseeching thee to give us grace so to follow the example of their stedfastness in thy faith, and obedience to thy holy commandments, that at the day of the general Resurrection, we, with all those who are of the mystical body of thy Son, may be set on his right hand, and hear that his most joyful voice: Come, ye blessed of my Father, inherit the kingdom prepared for you from the foundation of the world. Grant this, O Father, for the sake of the same, thy Son Jesus Christ, our only Mediator and Advocate. *Amen.*

Inasmuch as it may sometimes be expedient to say under shelter of the Church the whole or a part of the service appointed to be said at the Grave, the same is hereby allowed for weighty cause.

It is to be noted that this Office is appropriate to be used only for the faithful departed in Christ, provided that in any other case the Minister may, at his discretion, use such part of this Office, or such devotions taken from other parts of this Book, as may be fitting.

AT THE BURIAL OF THE DEAD AT SEA

The same Office may be used; but instead of the Sentence of Committal, the Minister shall say,

UNTO Almighty God we commend the soul of our *brother* departed, and we commit *his* body to the deep; in sure and certain hope of the Resurrection unto eternal life, through our Lord Jesus Christ; at whose coming in glorious majesty to judge the world, the sea shall give up her dead; and the corruptible bodies of those who sleep in him shall be changed, and made like unto his glorious body; according to the mighty working whereby he is able to subdue all things unto himself.

THE PRESBYTERIAN SERVICE

From *The Book of Common Worship* [1]

The Minister, meeting the Body at the entrance of the church and going before it up the aisle, or standing beside it if at the home, shall begin the service with one or more of these Sentences from the Holy Scriptures:

I AM the resurrection, and the life: he that believeth in me, though he were dead, yet shall he live: and whosoever liveth and believeth in me shall never die.

Our help is in the name of the Lord, who made heaven and earth.

Like as a father pitieth his children, so the Lord pitieth them that fear him.

Thou wilt keep him in perfect peace, whose mind is stayed on thee: because he trusteth in thee.

Thou wilt shew me the path of life: in thy presence is fulness of joy; at thy right hand there are pleasures for evermore.

Lord, to whom shall we go? Thou hast the words of eternal life.

[1] Revised edition; copyright, 1932, by the Board of Christian Education of the Presbyterian Church in the U. S. A.

AT THE BURIAL OF A CHILD

H<small>E</small> shall feed his flock like a shepherd: he shall gather the lambs with his arm, and carry them in his bosom.

Then let the Minister say:

Let us pray.

Then shall he lead the People in the Invocation, ending with The Lord's Prayer.

O<small>UR</small> Father in heaven, whose love is infinite and in whose will is our peace; be pleased to look down upon our sorrow, and enable us so to hear Thy holy Word, that through patience and comfort of the Scriptures we may have hope. And grant us the consolation of Thy Holy Spirit, that we may be raised above the shadows of mortality into the light of Thy countenance and the joy of Thy presence, through Him who died and rose again and ever liveth with Thee, even Jesus Christ our Lord. *Amen.*

O<small>UR</small> Father, who art in heaven, Hallowed be thy Name. Thy kingdom come. Thy will be done, On earth as it is in heaven. Give

us this day our daily bread.   And forgive us our
debts, As we forgive our debtors.   And lead us
not into temptation, But deliver us from evil:
For thine is the kingdom, and the power, and
the glory, for ever.   *Amen.*

*Then let one or more of the following Psalms be
chanted or read, closing with the* Gloria Patri:

From Psalm 90

LORD, thou hast been our dwelling place in all
generations.

Before the mountains were brought forth, or
ever thou hadst formed the earth and the world,
even from everlasting to everlasting, thou art
God.

For a thousand years in thy sight are but as
yesterday when it is past, and as a watch in the
night.

Thou carriest them away as with a flood;
they are as a sleep: in the morning they are like
grass which groweth up.

In the morning it flourisheth, and groweth
up; in the evening it is cut down, and withereth.

The days of our years are threescore years
and ten; and if by reason of strength they be
fourscore years; yet is their strength labor and

sorrow; for it is soon cut off, and we fly away.

So teach us to number our days, that we may apply our hearts unto wisdom.

O satisfy us early with thy mercy; that we may rejoice and be glad all our days.

Let thy work appear unto thy servants, and thy glory unto their children.

And let the favor of the Lord our God be upon us: and establish thou the work of our hands upon us; yea, the work of our hands establish thou it.

From Psalm 130

O UT of the depths have I cried unto thee, O Lord.

Lord, hear my voice: let thine ears be attentive to the voice of my supplications.

If thou, Lord, shouldest mark iniquities, O Lord, who shall stand?

But there is forgiveness with thee, that thou mayest be feared.

I wait for the Lord, my soul doth wait, and in his word do I hope.

My soul waiteth for the Lord more than they that watch for the morning: I say, more than they that watch for the morning.

From Psalm 46

GOD is our refuge and strength, a very present help in trouble.

Therefore will not we fear, though the earth be removed, and though the mountains be carried into the midst of the sea;

Though the waters thereof roar and be troubled, though the mountains shake with the swelling thereof.

There is a river, the streams whereof shall make glad the city of God, the holy place of the tabernacles of the most High.

God is in the midst of her; she shall not be moved: God shall help her, and that right early.

The Lord of hosts is with us: the God of Jacob is our refuge.

Psalm 121

I WILL lift up mine eyes unto the hills: from whence shall my help come?

My help cometh from the Lord, who made heaven and earth.

He will not suffer thy foot to be moved: he that keepeth thee will not slumber.

Behold, he that keepeth Israel will neither slumber nor sleep.

The Lord is thy keeper: the Lord is thy shade upon thy right hand.

The sun shall not smite thee by day, nor the moon by night.

The Lord will preserve thee from all evil: he will preserve thy soul.

The Lord will preserve thy going out and thy coming in, from this time forth, and even for evermore.

Psalm 23

THE Lord is my shepherd: I shall not want.
He maketh me to lie down in green pastures: he leadeth me beside the still waters.

He restoreth my soul: he leadeth me in the paths of righteousness for his name's sake.

Yea, though I walk through the valley of the shadow of death, I will fear no evil: for thou art with me; thy rod and thy staff they comfort me.

Thou preparest a table before me in the presence of mine enemies: thou anointest my head with oil; my cup runneth over.

Surely goodness and mercy shall follow me all the days of my life: and I will dwell in the house of the Lord for ever.

AT THE CLOSE OF THE PSALTER

Glory be to the Father, and to the Son: and to the Holy Ghost;

As it was in the beginning, is now, and ever shall be: world without end. *Amen.*

A Hymn or Anthem may here be sung.

Then let the Minister read from the Holy Scriptures, choosing if he will from the following passages, and before the reading let him say,

Hear the Word of God as written for our admonition and comfort.

St. John 14:1-3, 15-20, 25-27

LET not your heart be troubled: ye believe in God, believe also in me. In my Father's house are many mansions; if it were not so, I would have told you. I go to prepare a place for you. And if I go and prepare a place for you, I will come again, and receive you unto myself; that where I am, there ye may be also.

If ye love me, keep my commandments. And I will pray the Father, and he shall give you another Comforter, that he may abide with you for ever; even the Spirit of truth; whom the world cannot receive, because it seeth him not, neither knoweth him: but ye know him; for he dwelleth with you, and shall be in you. I will not leave you comfortless: I will come to you. Yet a little while, and the world seeth me no more; but ye see me: because I live, ye shall live also. At that day ye shall know that I am in my Father, and ye in me, and I in you.

These things have I spoken unto you, being yet present with you. But the Comforter, which is the Holy Ghost, whom the Father will send in my name, he shall teach you all things, and bring all things to your remembrance, whatsoever I have said unto you. Peace I leave with you, my peace I give unto you: not as the world giveth, give I unto you. Let not your heart be troubled, neither let it be afraid.

Romans 8:14-19, 22-25, 28, 31-35, 37-39

As many as are led by the Spirit of God, they are the sons of God. For ye have not received the spirit of bondage again to fear; but ye have received the Spirit of adoption, whereby we cry, Abba, Father. The Spirit itself beareth witness with our spirit, that we are the children of God: And if children, then heirs; heirs of God, and joint heirs with Christ;

if so be that we suffer with him, that we may be also glorified together.

For I reckon that the sufferings of this present time are not worthy to be compared with the glory which shall be revealed in us. For the earnest expectation of the creature waiteth for the manifestation of the sons of God. For we know that the whole creation groaneth and travaileth in pain together until now. And not only they, but ourselves also, which have the firstfruits of the Spirit, even we ourselves groan within ourselves, waiting for the adoption, to wit, the redemption of our body. For we are saved by hope: but hope that is seen is not hope: for what a man seeth, why doth he yet hope for? But if we hope for that we see not, then do we with patience wait for it.

And we know that all things work together for good to them that love God, to them who are the called according to his purpose. What shall we then say to these things? If God be for us, who can be against us? He that spared not his own Son, but delivered him up for us all, how shall he not with him also freely give us all things? Who shall lay any thing to the charge of God's elect? It is God that justifieth. Who is he that condemneth? It is Christ that died, yea rather, that is risen again, who is even at the right hand of God, who also maketh intercession for us.

Who shall separate us from the love of Christ? shall tribulation, or distress, or persecution, or famine, or nakedness, or peril, or sword? Nay, in all these things we are more than conquerors through him that loved us. For I am persuaded that neither death, nor life, nor angels, nor principalities, nor powers, nor things present, nor things to come, nor height, nor depth, nor any other creature, shall be able to separate us from the love of God, which is in Christ Jesus our Lord.

I Corinthians 15:20-28, 35-49, 54-58

Now is Christ risen from the dead, and become the firstfruits of them that slept. For since by man came death, by man came also the resurrection of the dead. For as in Adam all die, even so in Christ shall all be made alive. But every man in his own order: Christ the firstfruits; afterward they that are Christ's at his coming.

Then cometh the end, when he shall have delivered up the kingdom to God, even the Father; when he shall have put down all rule, and all authority and power. For he must reign, till he hath put all enemies under his feet. The last enemy that shall be destroyed is death. For he hath put all things under his feet. But when he saith, All things are put under him, it is manifest that he is excepted, which did put all things under him. And when all things shall be subdued unto him, then shall the Son also himself be subject unto him that put all things under him, that God may be all in all.

But some man will say, How are the dead raised up? and with what body do they come? Thou foolish one, that which thou sowest is not quickened, except it die. And that which thou sowest, thou sowest not that body that shall be, but bare grain, it may chance of wheat, or of some other grain: but God giveth it a body as it hath pleased him, and to every seed his own body. All flesh is not the same flesh: but there is one kind of flesh of men, another flesh of beasts, another of fishes, and another of birds. There are also celestial bodies, and bodies terrestrial: but the glory of the celestial is one, and the glory of the terrestrial is another. There is one glory of the sun, and another glory of the moon, and another glory of the stars; for one star differeth from another star in glory. So also is the resurrection of the dead. It is sown in corruption, it is raised in incorruption: it is sown in dishonor, it is raised in glory: it is sown in weakness, it is raised in power: it is sown a natural body, it is raised a spiritual body. There is a natural body, and there is a spiritual body. Howbeit that was not first which is spiritual, but that which is natural and afterward that which is spiritual. The first man is of the earth, earthy; the second man is the Lord from heaven. As is the earthy, such are they also that are earthy; and as is the heavenly, such are they also that are heavenly. And as we have borne the image of the earthy, we shall also bear the image of the heavenly.

So when this corruptible shall have put on incorruption, and this mortal shall have put on immortality, then shall be brought to pass the saying that is written, Death is swallowed up in victory. O death, where is thy sting? O grave, where is thy victory? The sting of death is sin; and the strength of sin is the law. But thanks be to God, which giveth us the victory through our Lord Jesus Christ. Therefore, my beloved brethren, be ye steadfast, unmovable, always abounding in the work of the Lord, forasmuch as ye know that your labor is not in vain in the Lord.

II Corinthians 4:15-5:10

ALL things are for your sakes, that the abundant grace might through the thanksgiving of many redound to the glory of God. For which cause we faint not; but though our outward man perish, yet the inward man is renewed day by day. For our light affliction, which is but for a moment, worketh for us a far more exceeding and eternal weight of glory; while we look not at the things which are seen, but at the things which are not seen: for the things which are seen are temporal; but the things which are not seen are eternal.

For we know that, if our earthly house of this tabernacle were dissolved, we have a building of God, a house not made with hands, eternal in the heavens. For in this we groan, earnestly desiring to be clothed upon with our house which is from heaven: if so be that being clothed we shall not be found naked. For we that are in this tabernacle do groan, being burdened: not for that we would be unclothed, but clothed upon, that mortality might be swallowed up of life. Now he that hath wrought us for the self-same thing is God, who also hath given unto us the earnest of the Spirit. Therefore we are always confident, knowing that, whilst we are at home in the body, we are absent from the Lord: (for we walk by faith, not by sight:) we are confident, I say, and willing rather to be absent from the body, and to be present with the Lord. Wherefore we labor, that, whether present or absent, we may be accepted of him. For we must all appear before the judgment seat of Christ; that every one may receive the things done in his body, according to that he hath done, whether it be good or bad.

I Thessalonians 4:13-18

BUT I would not have you to be ignorant, brethren, concerning them which are asleep, that ye sorrow not, even as others which have no hope. For if we believe that Jesus died and rose again, even so them also which sleep in Jesus will God bring with him. For this we say unto you by the word of the Lord, that we which are alive and remain unto the coming of the Lord shall not prevent them which are asleep. For the Lord himself shall descend from heaven with a shout, with the voice of the archangel, and with the trump of God: and the dead in Christ shall rise first: then we which are alive and remain shall be caught up together with them in the clouds, to meet the Lord in the air: and so shall we ever be with the Lord. Wherefore comfort one another with these words.

Revelation 21:1–4, 22–22:7

A<small>ND</small> I saw a new heaven and a new earth: for the first heaven and the first earth were passed away; and there was no more sea.

And I John saw the holy city, new Jerusalem, coming down from God out of heaven, prepared as a bride adorned for her husband. And I heard a great voice out of heaven, saying, Behold, the tabernacle of God is with men, and he will dwell with them, and they shall be his people, and God himself shall be with them, and be their God. And God shall wipe away all tears from their eyes: and there shall be no more death, neither sorrow, nor crying, neither shall there be any more pain: for the former things are passed away.

And I saw no temple therein: for the Lord God Almighty and the Lamb are the temple of it. And the city had no need of the sun, neither of the moon, to shine in it: for the glory of God did lighten it, and the Lamb is the light thereof. And the nations of them which are saved shall walk in the light of it: and the kings of the earth do bring their glory and honor into it. And the gates of it shall not be shut at all by day: for there shall be no night there. And they shall bring the glory and honor of the nations into it. And there shall in no wise enter into it anything that defileth, neither whatsoever worketh abomination, or maketh a lie; but they which are written in the Lamb's book of life.

And he showed me a pure river of water of life, clear as crystal, proceeding out of the throne of God and of the Lamb. In the midst of the street of it, and on either side of the river, was there the tree of life, which bare twelve manner of fruits, and yielded her fruit every month: and the leaves of the tree were for the healing of the nations. And there shall be no more curse: but the throne of God and of the Lamb shall be in it; and his servants shall serve him: And they shall see his face; and his name shall be in their foreheads. And there shall be no night there: and they need no candle, neither light of the sun; for the Lord God giveth them light: and they shall reign for ever and ever. And he said unto me, These sayings are faithful and true: and the Lord God of the holy prophets sent his angel to shew unto his servants the things which must shortly be done.

Behold, I come quickly: blessed is he that keepeth the sayings of the prophecy of this book.

AT THE BURIAL OF A CHILD

St. Matthew 18:1-5, 10, 14

A T the same time came the disciples unto Jesus, saying, Who is the greatest in the kingdom of heaven? And Jesus called a little child unto him, and set him in the midst of them, And said, Verily I say unto you, Except ye be converted, and become as little children, ye shall not enter into the kingdom of heaven. Whosoever therefore shall humble himself as this little child, the same is greatest in the kingdom of heaven. And whoso shall receive one such little child in my name receiveth me.

Take heed that ye despise not one of these little ones; for I say unto you, That in heaven their angels do always behold the face of my Father which is in heaven.

Even so it is not the will of your Father which is in heaven, that one of these little ones should perish.

St. Mark 10:13-16

AND they brought young children to him, that he should touch them: and his disciples rebuked those that brought them. But when Jesus saw it, he was much displeased, and said unto them, Suffer the little children to come unto me, and forbid them not: for of such is the kingdom of God. Verily I say unto you, Whosoever shall not receive the kingdom of God as a little child, he shall not enter therein. And he took them up in his arms, put his hands upon them, and blessed them.

And at the close of the reading from the Holy Scriptures the Minister may say:

THE Lord gave, and the Lord hath taken away: blessed be the Name of the Lord.

If it be thought desirable, an Address may here be made.

Then a Hymn may be sung, or may be read by the Minister.

Then the People, standing, may join with the Minister in their Confession of Faith.

I BELIEVE in God the Father Almighty, Maker of heaven and earth:
  And in Jesus Christ his only Son, our Lord:

Who was conceived by the Holy Ghost, Born of the Virgin Mary: Suffered under Pontius Pilate, Was crucified, dead, and buried: He descended into hell: [2] The third day He arose again from the dead: He ascended into heaven, And sitteth on the right hand of God the Father Almighty: From thence He shall come to judge the quick and the dead.

I believe in the Holy Ghost: The Holy Catholic Church; The Communion of Saints: The Forgiveness of sins: The Resurrection of the body: and the Life everlasting. *Amen.*

Then let the Minister say:

Let us pray.

The Minister may, if he so desire, use any of the following Prayers, having regard to the present circumstances.

FOR COMFORT

O LORD our God, help us as we seek to raise our thoughts from this changeful life to the calm eternity in which Thou dwellest, and to those things which know no change, save from glory to glory. Our weakness appeals to

---

[2] *I.e., He continued in the state of the dead until the third day.*

Thy pity. Hold not Thy peace at our tears. Lead us to the Rock that is higher than we. Lift us out of our disappointed purposes and broken hopes into the peace of Thy holy and blessed will. Our spirits turn to Thee in humble trust. Amid the decay of visible things, draw nigh unto our fainting souls, O Thou invisible Comforter. As the changes of life leave us poorer and sadder, may we know more of the constancy of Thy love, and the unfailing riches of Thy sympathy, whereof we have learned through Jesus our Saviour. *Amen.*

O FATHER, who in Thy grace dost give us the companions of our hearts and unite them to us with bonds of undying love, comfort Thy sorrowing children. May they think of their beloved as still with Thee. Let the memory of saintly lives strengthen their faith and hope and love. Grant them grace to return with courage to their home and work, and to discharge their duties with fidelity to Thee and loyalty to those whose trust and affection they share. Enable them to serve their generation with patience and devotion as fellow-citizens with the saints in light, and unite them with those who before have entered into Thine eternal city, through Jesus Christ, the Way, the Truth, and the Life. *Amen*.

O GOD, Thou helper of the helpless, look upon us in our sorrow. With Thy tender mercy sustain and comfort every mourning heart. Give us strength to return to the quiet duties of our place. With better aspirations, with truer diligence, with less trust in ourselves and more rest in Thee, may we dedicate ourselves anew to the service of Thy will; that, in the faith and spirit of Him who was made perfect through suffering, each of us may be ready to say, whenever the hour shall strike, "Father, I have finished the work which Thou gavest me to do." *Amen*.

O LORD and Saviour, we beseech Thee to comfort these Thy servants in their present sorrow; and as Thou didst send the Holy Spirit to be the Comforter of Thy people, strengthen them by the manifestation of His gracious indwelling, that they may be enabled to contemplate the joy of that better home, where Thy redeemed in everlasting light behold and worship Thee, who dwellest with the

Father, in the unity of the same Spirit, one God, world without end. *Amen.*

FOR THE COMFORT OF CHRIST'S PRESENCE

O LORD and Master, who Thyself didst weep beside the grave, and art touched with the feeling of our sorrows; fulfil now Thy promise that Thou wilt not leave Thy people comfortless, but wilt come to them. Reveal Thyself unto Thine afflicted servants, and cause them to hear Thee say, "I am the resurrection and the life." Help them, O Lord, to turn to Thee with true discernment, and to abide in Thee through living faith; that, finding now the comfort of Thy presence, they may have also a sure confidence in Thee for all that is to come: until the day break, and these shadows flee away. Hear us for Thy great mercy's sake, O Jesus Christ our Lord. *Amen.*

FOR THOSE BEREAVED

MOST merciful God, the consolation of the sorrowful and the support of the weary; look down in tender love and pity, we beseech Thee, upon Thy bereaved servants, whose joy is turned into mourning; so that, while they mourn, they may not murmur; but, remembering all Thy mercies, Thy promises, and Thy love in Christ, may resign themselves meekly into Thy hands, to be taught by Thee. Convert them wholly to Thyself, and fill their desolate hearts with Thy love, that they may cleave more closely to Thee, who bringest life out of death, and who canst turn their grief into eternal joy; through Jesus Christ our Lord. *Amen.*

AT THE BURIAL OF A CHILD

O LORD Jesus Christ, who didst take little children into Thine arms and bless them; open Thou our eyes, we beseech Thee, to perceive that it is of Thy goodness that Thou hast taken this Thy child into the everlasting arms of Thine infinite love; who livest and reignest with the Father and the Holy Spirit, world without end. *Amen.*

O GOD, whose ways are hidden and Thy works most wonderful, who makest nothing in vain and lovest all that Thou hast made; comfort Thou Thy servants, whose hearts are sore smitten and oppressed; and grant that they may so love and serve Thee in this life, that together with this Thy child, they may obtain the fulness of Thy promises in the world to come; through Jesus Christ our Lord. *Amen.*

IN CHRISTIAN HOPE AND TRIUMPH

THANKS be to Thee, O God, that Thy Son, Jesus Christ our Lord, conquered death and brought life and immortality to light through the gospel. We praise Thee for His assurance of Thy house of many mansions, where He has prepared a place for us, that where He is, there we may be also. We bless Thee for His promise to one of those who died beside Him upon a cross, that he should be with Him that day in Paradise. We thank Thee, above all, for our Lord's glorious resurrection from the dead, and for the sure hope of life with Him for evermore. Wherefore we rejoice in this hour for those whom we have lost on earth, but who are now with Thee. Though we sorrow for our loss, we bless Thee for their infinite gain, knowing that for them to be with Christ is far better. By Thy grace comfort our hearts with the thought of their safety and joy, and help us so to walk before Thee in faith and love, that in Thy good time, we may be joined to them in Thy heavenly presence evermore; through Jesus Christ our Lord. *Amen.*

O UR Father, unto Thee, in the light of our Saviour's blessed life, we would lift our souls. We thank Thee for that true light shining in our world with still increasing brightness. We thank Thee for all who have walked therein, and especially for those near to us and dear, in whose lives we have seen this excellent glory and beauty. May we know that in the body and out of the body they are with Thee, and that when these earthly days come to an end, it is not that our service of Thee and of one another may cease, but that it may begin anew. Make us glad in all who have faithfully lived; make us glad in all who have peacefully died. Lift us into light and love and purity and blessedness, and give us at last our portion with those who have trusted in Thee and sought, in small things as in great, in things temporal and eternal, to do Thy holy will. *Amen.*

FOR RESIGNATION

O LORD God, our heavenly Father, who alone art the Author and the Disposer of our life, from whom our spirits have come, and to whom they shall return; we acknowledge Thy sovereign power and right both to give and to take away, as seemeth good in Thy sight; and we most humbly beseech Thee, that unto all Thy righteous dealings we may yield ourselves with due resignation and patience; being assured that though we understand not the mystery of Thy ways, yet always in faithfulness, O Lord, dost Thou afflict us, and for Thy mercy's sake; through Jesus Christ our Lord. *Amen.*

FOR THE RIGHT USE OF AFFLICTION

O GOD, whose days are without end, and whose mercies cannot be numbered; make us deeply sensible of the shortness and uncertainty of human life, and let Thy Holy Spirit lead us through this present world in holiness and righteousness all the days of our life; that, when we shall have served Thee in our generation, we may be gathered unto our fathers, having the testimony of a good conscience; in the communion of Thy holy Church; in the confidence of a certain faith; in the comfort of a reasonable, religious and holy hope; in favor with Thee, our God; and in perfect charity with the world. All which we ask through Jesus Christ our Lord. *Amen.*

IN THANKSGIVING FOR GOD'S GRACE
TO THE DEPARTED

O GOD, who art the strength of Thy saints and who redeemest the souls of Thy servants; we bless Thy Name for all those who have died in the Lord, and who now rest from their labors, having received the end of their faith, even the salvation of their souls. Especially we call to remembrance Thy loving-kindness and Thy tender mercies to this Thy servant. For all Thy goodness that withheld not *his* portion in the joys of this earthly life, and for Thy guiding hand along the way of *his* pilgrimage; we give Thee thanks and praise. Especially we bless Thee for Thy grace that kindled in *his* heart the love of Thy dear Name; that enabled *him* to fight the good fight, to endure unto the end, and to obtain the victory; yea, to become more than conqueror, through Him that loveth us. We magnify Thy holy Name that *his* trials and temptations being ended, sickness and death being passed, with all the dangers and difficulties of this mortal life, *his* spirit is at home in Thy presence, at whose right hand dwelleth eternal peace. And grant, O Lord, we beseech Thee, that we who rejoice in the triumph of Thy saints may profit by their example, that becoming followers of their faith and patience, we also may enter with them into an inheritance incorruptible and undefiled, and that fadeth not away; through Jesus Christ our Lord. *Amen*.

FOR GRACE TO IMITATE THE RIGHTEOUS DEAD

ALMIGHTY and ever-living God, we yield unto Thee most high praise and hearty thanks for the wonderful grace and virtue declared in all Thy saints, who have been the choice vessels of Thy favor, and the lights of the world in their several generations; most humbly beseeching Thee to give us grace so to follow the example of their steadfastness in Thy faith, and obedience to Thy holy commandments, that we may hold fast to them by the pure bonds of Thy holy service and hereafter may be united with them in Thy heavenly kingdom; through Jesus Christ our Lord. *Amen*.

O LORD, we pray Thee, give us Thy strength that we may live more bravely and faithfully for the sake of those who are no longer with us here upon earth; and grant us so to serve Thee day by day that we may find eternal fellowship with them, through Him who died and rose again for us all, Jesus Christ our Lord. *Amen.*

FOR GRACE TO LIVE COURAGEOUSLY

Most loving Father, who willest Thy children to dread nothing but the loss of Thee and to cast all our care on Thee who carest for us; preserve us from faithless doubts and anxieties, and grant that no clouds of this mortal life may hide from us the light of Thine unchanging love. Renew within us, we beseech Thee, all joy and peace in believing, that we may ever abound in hope by the power of Thy Holy Spirit, and show forth our thankfulness to Thee in trustful and courageous lives; through Jesus Christ our Lord and Saviour. *Amen.*

FOR ENDURANCE UNTO THE END

O God, Thou King eternal, immortal, and invisible, the blessed and only Potentate; may we, who cannot see Thee with the eye of flesh, behold Thee steadfastly with the eye of faith, that we may not faint under the manifold trials and temptations of this mortal life, but endure as seeing Thee who art invisible; and grant that having fulfilled Thy will upon earth, we may behold Thy face in heaven, and be made partakers of those things which Thou hast promised to them who love Thy Son Jesus Christ our Lord, and wait His appearing; for whose sake, we beseech Thee to hear us; and unto whom, with Thee the Father and the Holy Spirit, we ascribe all glory and praise, for ever and ever. *Amen.*

FOR THOSE DEAR TO US

O THOU who hast ordered this wondrous world and who knowest all things in earth and heaven; so fill our hearts with trust in Thee, that by night and by day, at all times and in all seasons, we may without fear commit those who are dear to us to Thy never-failing love for this life and the life to come. *Amen.*

FOR GOD'S SUPPORT

O LORD, support us all the day long of this troublous life, until the shadows lengthen and the evening comes, and the busy world is hushed, and the fever of life is over, and our work is done. Then of Thy mercy grant us a safe lodging, and a holy rest, and peace at the last; through Jesus Christ our Lord. *Amen.*

A GENERAL PRAYER

O GOD our Father, from whom we come, unto whom we return, and in whom, while we tarry here, we live and move and have our being; we praise Thee for Thy good gift of life; for its wonder and mystery; its interests and joys; its friendships and fellowships. We thank Thee for the ties that bind us one to another. We bless Thee for Thy loving and patient dealings with us, whereby Thou dost ever teach us Thy truth and Thy way, by the varied experiences through which we pass; for the meanings that lie hidden even in the very heart of sorrow, pain, disappointment, loss, and grief; and for Thy guiding hand along the way of our pilgrimage.

We give thanks to Thee for this, Thy child, recalling all in *him* that made others love *him*. We bless Thee for all good and gracious influences in *his* home and training, for all that ministered to *his* best life. We thank Thee for all goodness and truth that has passed from *his* life into the lives of others, and has made the world richer for *his* presence. (*Here may be made mention of characteristics or service.*)

We bless Thy name for the revelation of

Thyself and of Thy love in our Lord Jesus Christ, and for the hope set before us in the gospel. We thank Thee that deep in the human heart is an unquenchable trust that life does not end with death; that the Father, who has made us, will not leave us in the dust, but will care for us beyond the bounds of vision, even as He has cared for us in this our earthly life. We praise Thy name that this our hope has been so wondrously confirmed in the life and words and resurrection of our Lord and Saviour, Jesus Christ.

Grant us, we beseech Thee, the comfort of Thine assured presence, and the quiet ministries of Thy Holy Spirit. Renew within us the great gifts of faith, patience, and enduring love. Help us to walk amid the things of this world with eyes open to the beauty and glory of the eternal; that so, among the sundry and manifold changes of this life, our hearts may surely there be fixed where true joys are to be found; through Jesus Christ our Lord. *Amen.*

THE BENEDICTION

THE peace of God, which passeth all understanding, keep your hearts and minds in the knowledge and love of God, and of His Son

Jesus Christ our Lord; and the blessing of God
Almighty, the Father, the Son, and the Holy
Spirit, be amongst you, and remain with you
always. *Amen*.

AT THE GRAVE

*When they are come to the grave, while the Body
of the Dead is made ready to be laid therein, let
the Minister say:*

OUR help is in the name of the Lord, who
made heaven and earth.

Like as a father pitieth his children, so the
Lord pitieth them that fear him.

For he knoweth our frame: he remembereth
that we are dust.

As for man, his days are as grass: as a flower
of the field, so he flourisheth.

For the wind passeth over it, and it is gone:
and the place thereof shall know it no more.

But the mercy of the Lord is from everlasting
to everlasting upon them that fear him, and his
righteousness unto children's children.

Or this:

I AM the resurrection and the life, saith the
Lord; he that believeth in me, though he
were dead, yet shall he live: and whosoever

liveth and believeth in me, shall never die

For we know that if our earthly house of this tabernacle were dissolved, we have a building of God, a house not made with hands, eternal in the heavens.

Then, while earth is cast upon the Body by some standing by, the Minister shall say:

FORASMUCH as Almighty God hath taken unto Himself the soul of our *brother* departed (*or*, the soul of this child), we therefore commit *his* body to the grave [3] (*earth to earth, ashes to ashes, dust to dust*); looking for the resurrection of the dead, and the life of the world to come, through our Lord Jesus Christ; who shall change our mortal body, that it may be made like unto His own glorious body; according to the mighty working whereby He is able to subdue all things unto Himself.

Then may be said or sung:

I HEARD a voice from heaven saying unto me, Write, Blessed are the dead who die in the Lord from henceforth: yea, saith the Spirit, that they may rest from their labors; and their works do follow them.

[3] *Or, his* body to the deep;
  Or, his ashes to their resting-place.

*Then the Minister shall offer one of the following
Prayers, or some other, and shall follow it with the
Lord's Prayer and the Benediction.*

O MERCIFUL God, the Father of our Lord
Jesus Christ, who is the resurrection and
the life; in whom whosoever believeth shall live,
though he die; we humbly beseech Thee to raise
us from the death of sin unto the life of righteousness; that, when we shall depart this life,
we may rest in Him; and at the last may be
found acceptable in Thy sight, and receive that
blessing which Thy Son shall pronounce to all
that love and serve Thee, saying, Come, ye
blessed of My Father, inherit the kingdom prepared for you from the foundation of the
world. Grant this, we beseech Thee, O merciful Father, through Jesus Christ, our Mediator
and Redeemer. *Amen.*

ETERNAL Love, with whom the souls of the
faithful, after they are freed from this
mortal flesh, shall abide for ever in strength and
gladness; we give Thee hearty thanks that their
bodies also, which have borne the image of the
earthy, shall bear the image of the heavenly.
Wherefore, having this confidence concerning
them that are asleep, we wait with cheerful hope

till Thou shalt accomplish the number of Thine elect; that we, with all that are departed in the true faith of Thy holy Name, may have our full salvation, both in body and soul, in Thine everlasting kingdom; through Him whose is the victory over death and the grave, even Jesus Christ our Lord. *Amen.*

Our Father, who art in heaven, Hallowed be thy Name. Thy kingdom come. Thy will be done, On earth as it is in heaven. Give us this day our daily bread. And forgive us our debts, As we forgive our debtors. And lead us not into temptation, But deliver us from evil: For thine is the kingdom, and the power, and the glory, for ever. *Amen.*

THE BENEDICTION

The grace of the Lord Jesus Christ, and the love of God, and the communion of the Holy Spirit, be with you all. *Amen.*

THE METHODIST SERVICE

From *The Ritual of The Methodist Church* [1]

The minister shall begin the service by reading one or more of the following sentences:

JESUS said, I am the resurrection, and the life: he that believeth in me, though he were dead, yet shall he live: and whosoever liveth and believeth in me shall never die.

The eternal God is thy refuge, and underneath are the everlasting arms.

The LORD is my light and my salvation; whom shall I fear? the LORD is the strength of my life; of whom shall I be afraid?

The righteous live forever, and the care of them is with the most High: with his right hand he shall cover them, and with his arm shall he shield them.

For we know that if our earthly house of this tabernacle were dissolved, we have a building of God, an house not made with hands, eternal in the heavens.

Then shall the minister say:

Let us pray.

[1] Copyright, 1944, by Whitmore & Stone.

Here may the minister offer one or both of the following prayers, ending with the Lord's Prayer.

ALMIGHTY God, fount of all life; thou art our refuge and strength; thou art our help in trouble. Enable us, we pray thee, to put our trust in thee, that we may obtain comfort, and find grace to help in this and every time of need; through Jesus Christ our Lord. *Amen.*

ALMIGHTY God, our Father, from whom we come, and unto whom our spirits return; thou hast been our dwelling place in all generations. Thou art our refuge and strength, a very present help in trouble. Grant us thy blessing in this hour, and enable us so to put our trust in thee that our spirits may grow calm and our hearts be comforted. Lift our eyes beyond the shadows of earth, and help us to see the light of eternity. So may we find grace and strength for this and every time of need; through Jesus Christ our Lord. *Amen.*

OUR Father who art in heaven, hallowed be thy name; thy kingdom come; thy will be done on earth as it is in heaven. Give us this day our daily bread. And forgive us our trespasses, as we forgive those who trespass against us. And lead us not into temptation, but deliver us from evil. For thine is the kingdom, and the power, and the glory, forever. *Amen.*

Here may be read one or more of these lessons from the Old Testament:

THE LORD is my shepherd; I shall not want. He maketh me to lie down in green pastures: he leadeth me beside the still waters.

He restoreth my soul: he leadeth me in the paths of righteousness for his name's sake.

Yea, though I walk through the valley of the shadow of death, I will fear no evil: for thou art with me; thy rod and thy staff they comfort me.

Thou preparest a table before me in the presence of mine enemies: thou anointest my head with oil; my cup runneth over.

Surely goodness and mercy shall follow me all the days of my life: and I will dwell in the house of the LORD forever.

LORD, thou has been our dwelling place in all generations.

Before the mountains were brought forth, or ever thou hadst formed the earth and the world, even from everlasting to everlasting, thou art God.

For a thousand years in thy sight are but as yesterday when it is past, and as a watch in the night.

Thou carriest them away as with a flood; they are as a sleep: in the morning they are like grass which groweth up.

In the morning it flourisheth, and groweth up; in the evening it is cut down, and withereth.

So teach us to number our days, that we may apply our hearts unto wisdom.

Let thy work appear unto thy servants, and thy glory unto their children.

And let the beauty of the LORD our God be upon us: and establish thou the work of our hands upon us; yea, the work of our hands establish thou it.

I WILL lift up mine eyes unto the hills, from whence cometh my help.

My help cometh from the LORD, who made heaven and earth.

He will not suffer thy foot to be moved: he that keepeth thee will not slumber.

Behold, he that keepeth Israel will neither slumber nor sleep.

The LORD is thy keeper: the LORD is thy shade upon thy right hand.

The LORD shall preserve thy going out and thy coming in from this time forth, and even for evermore.

THE LORD is my light and my salvation; whom shall I fear? The LORD is the strength of my life; of whom shall I be afraid?

Though an host should encamp against me, my heart shall not fear; though war should rise against me, in this will I be confident.

For in the time of trouble he shall hide me in his pavilion: in the secret of his tabernacle shall he hide me; he shall set me up upon a rock.

Teach me thy way, O LORD, and lead me in a plain path.

I had fainted, unless I had believed to see the goodness of the LORD in the land of the living.

Wait on the LORD: be of good courage, and he shall strengthen thine heart: wait, I say, on the LORD.

Here may be said or sung the Gloria Patri:

Glory be to the Father, and to the Son, and to the Holy Ghost; as it was in the beginning, s now, and ever shall be, world without end. *Amen.*

Here shall be read one or more of these lessons from the New Testament:

LET not your heart be troubled: ye believe in God, believe also in me. In my Father's house are many mansions: if it were not so, I would have told you. I go to prepare a place for you. And if I go and prepare a place for you, I will come again, and receive you unto myself; that where I am, there ye may be also. I am the way, the truth, and the life. If ye love me, keep my commandments. And I will pray the Father, and he shall give you another Comforter, that he may abide with you forever; even the Spirit of truth; whom the world cannot receive, because it seeth him not, neither knoweth him; but ye know him; for he dwelleth with you, and shall be in you. I will not leave you comfortless: I will come to you. Because I live, ye shall live also.

Peace I leave with you, my peace I give unto you: not as the world giveth, give I unto you. Let not your heart be troubled, neither let it be afraid.

As many as are led by the Spirit of God, they are the sons of God. For ye have not received the spirit of bondage again to fear; but ye have received the Spirit of adoption, whereby we cry, Abba, Father. The Spirit itself beareth witness with our spirit, that we are the children of God: and if children, then heirs; heirs of God, and joint heirs with Christ; if so be that we suffer with him, that we may be also glorified together.

For I reckon that the sufferings of this present time are not worthy to be compared with the glory which shall be revealed in us.

And we know that all things work together for good to them that love God.

What shall we then say to these things? If God be for us, who can be against us? Who shall separate us from the love of Christ? shall tribulation, or distress, or persecution, or famine, or nakedness, or peril, or sword? Nay, in all these things we are more than conquerors through him that loved us. For I am persuaded, that neither death, nor life, nor angels, nor principalities, nor powers, nor things present, nor things to come, nor height, nor depth, nor any other creature, shall be able to separate us from the love of God, which is in Christ Jesus our Lord.

Now is Christ risen from the dead, and become the firstfruits of them that slept.

But some man will say, How are the dead raised up? and with what body do they come? Thou fool, that which thou sowest is not quickened, except it die: but God giveth it a body as it has pleased him.

So also is the resurrection of the dead. It is sown in corruption; it is raised in incorruption:

It is sown in dishonor; it is raised in glory: it is sown in weakness; it is raised in power:

It is sown a natural body; it is raised a spiritual body. There is a natural body, and there is a spiritual body.

And as we have borne the image of the earthy, we shall also bear the image of the heavenly.

For this corruptible must put on incorruption, and this mortal must put on immortality. So when this corruptible shall have put on incorruption, and this mortal shall have put on immortality, then shall be brought to pass the saying that is written, Death is swallowed up in victory. O death, where is thy sting? O grave, where is thy victory? The sting of death is sin; and the strength of sin is the law. But thanks be to God, who giveth us the victory, through our Lord Jesus Christ. Therefore, my beloved brethren, be ye steadfast, unmovable, always abounding in the work of the Lord, forasmuch as ye know that your labor is not in vain in the Lord.

AND I John saw the holy city, new Jerusalem, coming down from God out of heaven, prepared as a bride adorned for her husband. And I heard a great voice out of heaven saying, Behold, the tabernacle of God is with men, and he will dwell with them, and they shall be his people, and God himself shall be with them, and be their God. And God shall wipe away all tears from their eyes; and there shall be no more death, neither sorrow, nor crying, neither shall there be any more pain: for the former things are passed away.

AND he showed me a pure river of water of life, clear as crystal, proceeding out of the throne of God and of the Lamb. In the midst of the street of it, and on either side of the river, was there the tree of life, which bare twelve manners of fruits, and yielded her fruit every month: and the leaves of the tree were for the healing of the nations. And there shall be no more curse: but the throne of God and of the Lamb shall be in it; and his servants shall serve him: and they shall see his face; and his name shall be in their foreheads. And there shall be no night there; and they need no candle, neither light of the sun; for the Lord God giveth them light: and they shall reign for ever and ever.

For this cause I bow my knees unto the Father of our Lord Jesus Christ, of whom the whole family in heaven and earth is named, that he would grant you, according to the riches of his glory, to be strengthened with might by his Spirit in the inner man; that Christ may dwell in your hearts by faith; that ye, being rooted and grounded in love, may be able to comprehend with all saints what is the breadth, and length, and depth, and height; and to know the love of Christ, which passeth knowledge, that ye might be filled with all the fullness of God. Now unto him that is able to do exceeding abundantly above all that we ask or think, according to the power that worketh in us, unto him be glory in the church by Christ

Jesus throughout all ages, world without end. *Amen.*

Here may follow music and an address, closing with extempore prayer, or one of the following prayers:

ETERNAL God, who committest to us the swift and solemn trust of life; since we know not what a day may bring forth, but only that the hour for serving thee is always present, may we wake to the instant claims of thy holy will, not waiting for tomorrow, but yielding today. Consecrate with thy presence the way our feet may go; and the humblest work will shine, and the roughest places be made plain. Lift us above unrighteous anger and mistrust into faith and hope and love by a simple and steadfast reliance on thy sure will. In all things draw us to the mind of Christ, that thy lost image may be traced again, and that thou mayest own us as at one with him and thee. *Amen.*

O GOD, who art the strength of thy saints, and who redeemest the souls of thy servants; we bless thy name for all those who have died in the Lord, and who now rest from their labors, having received the end of their faith, even the salvation of their souls. Especially we

call to remembrance thy lovingkindness and thy
tender mercies to this thy servant. For all thy
goodness that withheld not *his* portion in the
joys of this earthly life, and for thy guiding
hand along the way of *his* pilgrimage, we give
thee thanks and praise. Especially we bless thee
for thy grace that kindled in *his* heart the love
of thy dear name, that enabled *him* to fight the
good fight, to endure unto the end, and to obtain the victory, yea, to become more than conqueror, through him that loveth us. We magnify thy holy name that, *his* trials and temptations being ended, sickness and death being
passed, with all the dangers and difficulties of
this mortal life, *his* spirit is at home in thy presence, with whom dwelleth eternal peace. And
grant, O Lord, we beseech thee, that we who
rejoice in the triumph of thy saints may profit
by their example, that, becoming followers of
their faith and patience, we also may enter with
them into an inheritance incorruptible and undefiled, and that fadeth not away; through Jesus
Christ our Lord. *Amen.*

O GOD, the Lord of life, the Conqueror of
death, our help in every time of trouble,
who dost not willingly grieve or afflict the chil-

dren of men; comfort us who mourn, and give us grace, in the presence of death, to worship thee, that we may have sure hope of eternal life and be enabled to put our whole trust in thy goodness and mercy; through Jesus Christ our Lord. *Amen.*

FATHER of spirits, we have joy at this time in all who have faithfully lived, and in all who have peacefully died. We thank thee for all fair memories and all living hopes; for the sacred ties that bind us to the unseen world; for the dear and holy dead who compass us as a cloud of witnesses, and make the distant heaven a home to our hearts. May we be followers of those who now inherit the promises; through Jesus Christ our Lord. *Amen.*

O LORD and Master, who thyself didst weep beside the grave, and art touched with the feeling of our sorrows; fulfill now thy promise that thou wilt not leave thy people comfortless, but wilt come to them. Reveal thyself unto thy sorrowing servants, and cause them to hear thee say, I am the resurrection, and the life. Help them, O Lord, to turn to thee with true discernment, and to abide in thee through living faith, that, finding now the comfort of thy presence, they may have also a sure confidence in thee for all that is to come; until the day break, and the shadows flee away. Hear us for thy great mercy's sake, O Jesus Christ our Lord. *Amen.*

O THOU who hast ordered this wondrous world, and who knowest all things in earth and heaven; so fill our hearts with trust in thee that, by night and by day, at all times and in all seasons, we may without fear commit those who are dear to us to thy never-failing love for this life and the life to come. *Amen.*

O LORD, we pray thee, give us thy strength, that we may live more bravely and faithfully for the sake of those who are no longer with us here upon earth; and grant us so to serve thee day by day that we may find eternal fellowship with them; through him who died and rose again for us all, Jesus Christ our Lord. *Amen.*

ALMIGHTY God, who art leading us through the changes of time to the rest and blessedness of eternity; be thou near to comfort and uphold. Make us to know and feel that thy children are precious in thy sight, that they live evermore with thee, and that thy mercy endureth forever.　Thankful for the life which thou hast given us for these seasons, we pray thy help now to resign it obediently unto thee. Assist us to return to the scenes of our daily life, to obey thy will with patience, and to bear our trials with fortitude and hope.　And when the peace of death falls upon us, may we find our perfect rest in thee; through Jesus Christ our Lord.　*Amen.*

Then may the minister say:

THE LORD bless you, and keep you: the LORD make his face shine upon you, and be gracious unto you: the LORD lift up his countenance upon you, and give you peace.　*Amen.*

At the grave, when the people are assembled, the minister shall say:

OUR help is in the name of the LORD, who made heaven and earth.

Like as a father pitieth his children, so the LORD pitieth them that fear him.

Say to them that are of a fearful heart, Be

strong, fear not: behold, your God will come and save you.

The mercy of the LORD is from everlasting to everlasting upon them that fear him, and his righteousness unto children's children.

Then the minister may say:

FORASMUCH as the spirit of the departed has entered into the life immortal, we therefore commit *his* body to its resting place, but *his* spirit we commend to God, remembering how Jesus said upon the cross, "Father, into thy hands I commend my spirit."

Or the minister may say:

FORASMUCH as Almighty God hath received unto himself the soul of our departed *brother*, we therefore tenderly commit *his* body to the ground, in the blessed hope that as *he* hath borne the image of the earthly so also *he* shall bear the image of the heavenly.

Or the minister may say:

FORASMUCH as the spirit of the departed hath returned to God who gave it, we therefore commit *his* body to the ground, earth to earth, ashes to ashes, dust to dust; looking for the general resurrection in the last day, and the life of the world to come, through our Lord Jesus Christ; at whose coming in glorious majesty to judge the world, the earth and the sea shall give up their dead; and the corruptible bodies of those who sleep in him shall be changed and made like unto his own glorious body; according to the mighty working whereby he is able to subdue all things unto himself.

Then may be said:

I HEARD a voice from heaven, saying unto me: Blessed are the dead who die in the Lord from henceforth: Yea, saith the Spirit, that they may rest from their labors; and their works do follow them.

> Lord, have mercy upon us.
> *Christ, have mercy upon us.*
> Lord, have mercy upon us.

Here may the minister and people unite in the Lord's Prayer:

O UR Father who art in heaven, hallowed be thy name; thy kingdom come; thy will be done on earth as it is in heaven. Give us this day our daily bread. And forgive us our trespasses, as we forgive those who trespass against us. And lead us not into temptation, but deliver us from evil. For thine is the kingdom, and the power, and the glory, forever. *Amen*.

Then the minister may say one or more of the following prayers:

ALMIGHTY God, with whom do live the spirits of those who depart hence in the Lord, and with whom the souls of the faithful after death are in strength and gladness; we give thee hearty thanks for the good examples of all those thy servants who, having finished their course in faith, do now rest from their labor. And we beseech thee that we, with all those who have finished their course in faith, may have our perfect consummation and bliss in thy eternal and everlasting glory; through Jesus Christ our Lord. *Amen*.

O MERCIFUL God, the Father of our Lord Jesus Christ, who is the resurrection and the life, in whom whosoever believeth shall live, though he die, and whosoever liveth and believeth in him shall not die eternally; we meekly beseech thee, O Father, to raise us from the death of sin unto the life of righteousness, that when we shall depart this life we may rest in him, and may receive that blessing which thy well-beloved Son shall pronounce to all that love and fear thee, saying, Come, ye blessed of my Father, receive the kingdom prepared for you from the foundation of the world. Grant this, we beseech thee, O merciful Father, through Jesus Christ our Mediator and Redeemer. *Amen.*

O GOD of infinite compassion, who art the comforter of thy children; look down in thy tender love and pity, we beseech thee, upon thy servants. In the stillness of our hearts we entreat for them thy sustaining grace. Be thou their stay, their strength, and their shield, that trusting in thee they may know thy presence near, and in the assurance of thy love be delivered out of their distresses; through Jesus Christ our Lord. *Amen.*[2]

Then may the minister say:

THE grace of the Lord Jesus Christ, and the love of God, and the communion of the Holy Spirit, be with you all. *Amen.*

[2] Adapted by permission from *The Book of Common Order* (1932) of the United Church of Canada.

THE ORDER FOR THE BURIAL OF A CHILD

The minister shall begin the service by reading the following sentences:

JESUS said, I am the resurrection, and the life: he that believeth in me, though he were dead, yet shall he live: and whosoever liveth and believeth in me shall never die.

He shall feed his flock like a shepherd: he shall gather the lambs with his arm, and carry them in his bosom.

Blessed are the pure in heart: for they shall see God.

Then shall the minister say:

Let us pray.

Here may the minister offer one or both of the following prayers:

OUR heavenly Father, look upon us in our sorrow, and abide with us in our loneliness. O thou who makest no life in vain, and who lovest all that thou hast made, lift upon us the light of thy countenance and give us peace; through Jesus Christ our Lord. *Amen.*

O GOD our Father, we pray that thou wilt keep in tender love the life which we shall hold in blessed memory. Help us who continue here to serve thee with constancy, trusting in thy promise of eternal life, that hereafter we may be united with thy blessed children in glory everlasting; through Jesus Christ our Lord. *Amen.*

Here may be read:

THE Lord is my shepherd; I shall not want.
He maketh me to lie down in green pastures: he leadeth me beside the still waters.

He restoreth my soul: he leadeth me in the paths of righteousness for his name's sake.

Yea, though I walk through the valley of the shadow of death, I will fear no evil: for thou art with me; thy rod and thy staff, they comfort me.

Thou preparest a table before me in the presence of mine enemies: thou anointest my head with oil; my cup runneth over.

Surely goodness and mercy shall follow me all the days of my life: and I will dwell in the house of the LORD forever.

I WILL lift up mine eyes unto the hills; from whence cometh my help.

My help cometh from the LORD, who made heaven and earth.

He will not suffer thy foot to be moved: he that keepeth thee will not slumber.

Behold, he that keepeth Israel shall neither slumber nor sleep.

The LORD is thy keeper: the LORD is thy shade upon thy right hand.

The LORD shall preserve thy going out and thy coming in from this time forth, and even for evermore.

Here shall be read these lessons from the Gospel:

AT THE same time came the disciples unto Jesus, saying, Who is the greatest in the kingdom of heaven? And Jesus called a little child unto him, and set him in the midst of them, and said, Verily I say unto you, Except ye be converted, and become as little children, ye shall not enter into the kingdom of heaven. Whosoever therefore shall humble himself as this little child, the same is the greatest in the kingdom of heaven. And whoso shall receive one such little child in my name receiveth me.

Take heed that ye despise not one of these little ones; for I say unto you, That in heaven their angels do always behold the face of my Father which is in heaven.

Let not your heart be troubled: ye believe in God, believe also in me. In my Father's house are many mansions: if it were not so, I would have told you. I go to prepare a place for you. And if I go and prepare a place for you, I will come again, and receive you unto myself; that where I am, there ye may be also. I am the way, the truth, and the life. If ye love me, keep my commandments. And I will pray the Father, and he shall give you another Comforter, that he may abide with you forever; even the Spirit of truth; whom the world cannot receive, because it seeth him not, neither knoweth him; but ye know him; for he dwelleth with you, and shall be in you. I will not leave you comfortless: I will come to you. Because I live, ye shall live also.

Peace I leave with you, my peace I give unto you: not as the world giveth, give I unto you. Let not your heart be troubled, neither let it be afraid.

Here may follow music and an address, after which the minister shall say:

Let us pray.

Here may the minister offer extempore prayer or one or more of the following prayers:

O GOD, who art the Father of the families of the earth; look with compassion upon this bereaved family, and pour thy heavenly comfort into their hearts. Help them by faith to see this child, over whom they grieve, safe in that home where sin and sorrow cannot enter. Enrich with thy presence those who mourn; abide in their home; lift up their hearts; bless them with thy favor, which is better than life; and so guide them through the trials and temptations of this world that their reunited family may know fullness of joy in thy presence for evermore. Grant this through him who loved little children and blessed them, even thy Son Jesus Christ our Lord. *Amen.*

O MERCIFUL Father, whose face the angels of thy little ones do always behold in heaven; grant us steadfastly to believe that this thy child hath been taken into the safe keeping of thine eternal love; through Jesus Christ our Lord. *Amen.*

O GOD, who healest the broken in heart, and bindest up their wounds; look down in tender pity and compassion upon thy servants whose joy has been turned into mourning.

Leave them not comfortless, but grant that they may be drawn closer to one another by their common sorrow. As thou hast given them this new tie to bind them to the world unseen, so grant unto them that where their treasure is, there may their hearts be also. Fill their souls with the light and comfort of thy presence. Grant unto them such a vision of that life wherein all mysteries shall be revealed, and all tears be wiped away, that they may be able to endure as seeing thee who art invisible. So dwell with them and be their God, until the day break and the shadows flee away; through Jesus Christ our Lord. *Amen.*

Then may the minister say:

THE LORD bless you, and keep you: the LORD make his face shine upon you, and be gracious unto you: the LORD lift up his countenance upon you, and give you peace. *Amen.*

At the grave, when the people are assembled, the minister shall say:

JESUS saith to his disciples, Ye now therefore have sorrow: but I will see you again, and your heart shall rejoice, and your joy no man taketh from you.

FORASMUCH as the departed has entered into the life immortal, we therefore commit *his* body to its resting place, but *his* spirit we commend to God, remembering how Jesus said upon the cross, "Father, into thy hands I commend my spirit."

Then shall the minister say:

ALMIGHTY God, Father of our Lord Jesus Christ, who gave his life for our redemption, and who promised the Holy Spirit, the Comforter; strengthen, we beseech thee, the faith of these bereaved ones, that they may contemplate with peace the blessedness of that eternal home which thou hast prepared for all who love and serve thee. Grant that they, and all others whose joy is turned into mourning, cleaving more closely unto him who is the resurrection and the life, may be led by thy spirit through this uncertain life, till the day break and the shadows flee away. *Amen.*

O GOD, whose most dear Son did take little children into his arms and bless them; give us grace, we beseech thee, to entrust the soul of this child to thy never-failing care and love, and bring us all to thy heavenly kingdom;

through the same thy Son, Jesus Christ our Lord. *Amen.*

A LMIGHTY God, Father of mercies and giver of all comfort; deal graciously, we pray thee, with all those who mourn, that, casting every care on thee, they may know the consolation of thy love; through Jesus Christ our Lord. *Amen.*

Here the minister and the people may unite in the Lord's Prayer:

O UR Father who art in heaven, hallowed be thy name; thy kingdom come; thy will be done on earth as it is in heaven. Give us this day our daily bread. And forgive us our trespasses, as we forgive those who trespass against us. And lead us not into temptation, but deliver us from evil. For thine is the kingdom, and the power, and the glory, forever. *Amen.*

Then may the minister say:

T HE grace of the Lord Jesus Christ, and the love of God, and the communion of the Holy Spirit, be with you all. *Amen.*

PART II

ADDITIONAL LITURGICAL MATERIAL

PROCESSIONAL SENTENCES

THE souls of the righteous are in the hand of God, and there shall no evil touch them. They are in peace.

In his favour is life: weeping may endure for a night, but joy cometh in the morning.

Fear not; for I have redeemed thee, I have called thee by thy name; thou art mine. When thou passest through the waters, I will be with thee; and through the rivers, they shall not overflow thee: when thou walkest through the fire, thou shalt not be burned; neither shall the flame kindle upon thee. For I am the Lord thy God, the Holy One of Israel, thy Saviour.

LIKE as a father pitieth his children, so the Lord pitieth them that fear him. For he knoweth our frame; he remembereth that we are dust.

The eternal God is thy refuge, and underneath are the everlasting arms.

None of us liveth to himself, and no man dieth to himself. For whether we live, we live unto the Lord; and whether we die, we die unto the Lord: whether we live therefore, or die, we are the Lord's. For to this end Christ both died and rose, and revived, that he might be Lord both of the dead and living.

WE know that if our earthly house of this tabernacle were dissolved, we have a building of God, an house not made with hands, eternal in the heavens.

If any man be in Christ, he is a new creature: old things are passed away; behold, all things are become new.

I have fought a good fight, I have finished my course, I have kept the faith: henceforth there is laid up for me a crown of righteousness, which the Lord, the righteous judge, shall give me at that day: and not to me only, but unto all them also that love his appearing.

THE eternal God is thy refuge, and underneath are the everlasting arms.

Our help is in the name of the Lord, who made heaven and earth.

Jesus said, I am the resurrection, and the life: he that believeth in me, though he were dead yet shall he live: and whosoever liveth and believeth in me shall never die.

The righteous live forever, and the care of them is with the Most High: with his right hand he shall cover them, and with his arm shall he shield them.

AT THE FUNERAL OF A CHILD

HE shall feed his flock like a shepherd: he shall gather the lambs with his arm, and carry them in his bosom.

And they shall be mine, saith the Lord of hosts, in that day when I make up my jewels.

And the streets of the city shall be full of boys and girls playing in the streets thereof.

In heaven their angels do always behold the face of my Father which is in heaven.

I AM the resurrection and the life, saith the Lord: he that believeth in me, though he were dead, yet shall he live: and whosoever liveth and believeth in me, shall never die.

Jesus called them unto him and said, Suffer the little children to come unto me, and forbid them not: for of such is the kingdom of God.

He shall feed his flock like a shepherd: he shall gather the lambs with his arms, and carry them in his bosom.

INVOCATIONS

ETERNAL God, our Heavenly Father, who lovest us with an everlasting love, and canst turn the shadow of death into the morning; help us now to wait upon thee with reverent and submissive hearts. In the silence of this hour speak to us of eternal things, that through patience and comfort of the Scriptures we may hope, and be lifted above our darkness and distress into the light and peace of thy presence; through Jesus Christ our Lord. *Amen.*

ALMIGHTY God, our Heavenly Father, who art our Refuge and Strength, and a very present help in time of trouble; Enable us, we pray thee, to put our trust in thee, and seeing that we have an High Priest who is touched with the feeling of our infirmities, may we come boldly unto the throne of grace, that we may obtain mercy, and find grace to help in this time of need; through Jesus Christ our Lord. *Amen.*

O GOD, of light eternal, we look to thee. Though thy cloud is round about thee and the shadow lies upon us here, we know that thy mercy is undimmed; and with perfect trust we wait for thee, as they whose eyes watch for the morning. Do with us as thou wilt: call us to our work, or to our rest: bid us take our burden, or lay it down. We murmur not, O Lord. Only abide with us by night and day; and be our strength to do and bear thy perfect will. *Amen.*

—JAMES MARTINEAU

ALMIGHTY and everlasting God, the Lord of our life and death, we desire to acknowledge thee in all our ways, and in all the events which befall us. In sorrow of heart, yet in quietness and confidence, we have gathered for these last solemn and tender offices of faith and love. Lift us above the shadow and the sadness of mortality into the light of thy countenance and the comfort of thy presence. Speak to us thy word of peace, as we stand now in the presence of death. It is thine own hour. The loneliness and the silence thou hast made. But thou canst do thy children no harm. In sorrow as in joy, in loss as in gain, in life as in death, we confess thee to be good. Thou art the Lord of life; we trust in thee, through Christ. *Amen.*[1]

—JOHN HUNTER

O LORD, thou who art the Father of mercies, and the God of all comfort; look with compassion, we pray thee, upon all gathered here now, that our minds and hearts shall be at thy command. Grant that this service of holy comfort which we now hold in thy name may bring to all a sense of heavenly nearness and of great trust in thee. And may the peace of Christ the Saviour, even the peace that passeth all understanding, abide with us and rest upon all these dear ones. We pray through Jesus Christ our Lord. *Amen.*

—N. B. H., JR.

[1] From *Devotional Services.* Used by permission of the publisher and copyright owner, E. P. Dutton & Co.

READINGS FROM THE OLD TESTAMENT

Psalm 23 (Prayer Book Version)

THE Lord is my shepherd; therefore can I lack nothing.

He shall feed me in a green pasture, and lead me forth beside the waters of comfort.

He shall convert my soul, and bring me forth in the paths of righteousness for his Name's sake.

Yea, though I walk through the valley of the shadow of death, I will fear no evil; for thou art with me; thy rod and thy staff comfort me.

Thou shalt prepare a table before me against them that trouble me; thou hast anointed my head with oil, and my cup shall be full.

Surely thy loving-kindness and mercy shall follow me all the days of my life; and I will dwell in the house of the Lord for ever.

From Psalm 39

LORD, make me to know mine end, and the measure of my days, what it is; that I may know how frail I am.

Behold, thou hast made my days as an handbreadth; and mine age is as nothing before thee: verily every man at his best state is altogether vanity.

Surely every man walketh in a vain show; surely they are disquieted in vain: he heapeth up riches, and knoweth not who shall gather them.

And now, Lord, what wait I for? my hope is in thee.

Deliver me from all my transgressions: make me not the reproach of the foolish.

When thou with rebukes dost correct man for iniquity, thou makest his beauty to consume away like a moth: surely every man is vanity.

Hear my prayer, O Lord, and give ear unto my cry; hold not thy peace at my tears; for I am a stranger with thee, and a sojourner, as all my fathers were.

O spare me, that I may recover strength, before I go hence, and be no more.

From Psalm 103

Bless the Lord, O my soul: and all that is within me, bless his holy name.

Bless the Lord, O my soul, and forget not all his benefits:

Who forgiveth all thine iniquities; who healeth all thy diseases;

Who redeemeth thy life from destruction; who crowneth thee with lovingkindness and tender mercies;

Who satisfieth thy mouth with good things; so that thy youth is renewed like the eagle's.

He hath not dealt with us after our sins; nor rewarded us according to our iniquities.

For as the heaven is high above the earth, so great is his mercy toward them that fear him.

As far as the east is from the west, so far hath he removed our transgressions from us.

Like as a father pitieth his children, so the Lord pitieth them that fear him.

For he knoweth our frame; he remembereth that we are dust.

As for man, his days are as grass: as a flower of the field, so he flourisheth.

For the wind passeth over it, and it is gone; and the place thereof shall know it no more.

But the mercy of the Lord is from everlasting to everlasting upon them that fear him, and his righteousness unto children's children;

To such as keep his covenant, and to those that remember his commandments to do them.

From Psalm 116

I LOVE the Lord, because he hath heard my voice and my supplications.

Because he hath inclined his ear unto me, therefore will I call upon him as long as I live.

The sorrows of death compassed me, and the pains of hell gat hold upon me: I found trouble and sorrow.

Then called I upon the name of the Lord; O Lord, I beseech thee, deliver my soul.

Gracious is the Lord, and righteous; yea, our God is merciful.

The Lord preserveth the simple: I was brought low, and he helped me.

Return unto thy rest, O my soul; for the Lord hath dealt bountifully with thee.

For thou hast delivered my soul from death, mine eyes from tears, and my feet from falling.

What shall I render unto the Lord for all his benefits toward me?

I will take the cup of salvation, and call upon the name of the Lord.

Precious in the sight of the Lord is the death of his saints.

O Lord, truly I am thy servant; I am thy servant, and the son of thine handmaid: thou hast loosed my bonds.

I will offer to thee the sacrifice of thanksgiving, and will call upon the name of the Lord.

Isaiah 35:3-10

STRENGTHEN ye the weak hands, and confirm the feeble knees. Say to them that are of a fearful heart, Be strong, fear not: behold, your God will come with vengeance, even God with a recompence; he will come and save you. Then the eyes of the blind shall be opened, and the ears of the deaf shall be unstopped: then shall the lame man leap as an hart, and the tongue of the dumb sing: for in the wilderness shall waters break out, and streams in the desert. And the parched ground shall become a pool, and the thirsty land springs of water: in the habitation of dragons, where each lay, shall be grass with reeds and rushes. And an highway shall be there, and a way, and it shall be called The way of holiness; the unclean shall not pass over it; but it shall be for those: the wayfaring men, though fools, shall not err therein. No lion shall be there, nor any ravenous beast shall go up thereon, it shall not be found there; but the redeemed shall walk there. And the ransomed of the Lord shall return, and come to Zion with songs and everlasting joy upon their heads: they shall obtain joy and gladness, and sorrow and sighing shall flee away.

Isaiah 40:1-11, 28-31

COMFORT ye, comfort ye my people, saith your God. Speak ye comfortably to Jerusalem, and cry unto her, that her warfare is accomplished, that her iniquity is pardoned: for she hath received of the Lord's hand double for all her sins. The voice of him that crieth in the wilderness, Prepare ye the way of the Lord, make straight in the desert a highway for our God. Every valley shall be exalted, and every mountain and hill shall be made low: and the crooked shall be made straight, and the rough places plain: and the glory of the Lord shall be revealed, and all flesh shall see it together: for the mouth of the Lord hath spoken it. The voice said, Cry. And he said, What shall I cry? All flesh is grass, and all the goodliness thereof is as the flower of the field: the grass withereth, the flower fadeth: because the spirit of the Lord bloweth upon it: surely the people is grass. The grass withereth, the flower fadeth: but the word of our God shall stand for ever. O Zion, that bringest good tidings, get thee up into the high mountain; O Jerusalem, that bringest good tidings, lift up thy voice with strength; lift it up, be not afraid; say unto the cities of Judah, Behold your God!   Behold, the Lord God will come with strong hand, and his arm shall rule for him: behold, his reward is with him, and his work before him.   He shall feed his flock like a shepherd: he shall gather the lambs with his arm, and carry them in his bosom, and shall gently lead those that are with young.   Hast thou not known? hast thou not heard, that the everlasting God, the Lord, the Creator of the ends of the earth, fainteth not, neither is weary? there is no searching of his understanding.   He giveth power to the faint; and to them that have no might he increaseth strength.   Even the youths shall faint and be weary, and the young men shall utterly fall: But they that wait upon the Lord shall renew their strength; they shall mount up with wings as eagles; they shall run, and not be weary; and they shall walk, and not faint.

AT THE FUNERAL OF A GOOD MAN

Psalm 1

BLESSED is the man that walketh not in the counsel of the ungodly, nor standeth in the way of sinners, nor sitteth in the seat of the scornful:

But his delight is in the law of the Lord; and in his law doth he meditate day and night.

And he shall be like a tree planted by the rivers of water, that bringeth forth his fruit in his season; his leaf also shall not wither; and whatsoever he doeth shall prosper.

The ungodly are not so: but are like the chaff which the wind driveth away.

Therefore the ungodly shall not stand in the judgment, nor sinners in the congregation of the righteous.

For the Lord knoweth the way of the righteous: but the way of the ungodly shall perish.

Psalm 15

LORD, who shall abide in thy tabernacle? who shall dwell in thy holy hill?

He that walketh uprightly, and worketh righteousness, and speaketh the truth in his heart.

He that backbiteth not with his tongue, nor doeth evil to his neighbour, nor taketh up a reproach against his neighbour.

In whose eyes a vile person is contemned; but he honoureth them that fear the Lord. He that sweareth to his own hurt, and changeth not.

He that putteth not out his money to usury, nor taketh reward against the innocent. He that doeth these things shall never be moved.

AT THE FUNERAL OF A WORTHY MATRON

Proverbs 31:10-31

WHO can find a virtuous woman? for her price is far above rubies.

The heart of her husband doth safely trust in her, so that he shall have no need of spoil.

She will do him good and not evil all the days of her life.

She seeketh wool, and flax, and worketh willingly with her hands.

She is like the merchants' ships; she bringeth her food from afar.

She riseth also while it is yet night, and giveth meat to her household, and a portion to her maidens.

She considereth a field, and buyeth it: with the fruit of her hands she planteth a vineyard.

She girdeth her loins with strength, and strengtheneth her arms.

She perceiveth that her merchandise is good: her candle goeth not out by night.

She layeth her hands to the spindle, and her hands hold the distaff.

She stretcheth out her hand to the poor; yea, she reacheth forth her hands to the needy.

She is not afraid of the snow for her household: for all her household are clothed with scarlet.

She maketh herself coverings of tapestry; her clothing is silk and purple.

Her husband is known in the gates, when he sitteth among the elders of the land.

She maketh fine linen, and selleth it; and delivereth girdles unto the merchant.

Strength and honour are her clothing; and she shall rejoice in time to come.

She openeth her mouth with wisdom; and in her tongue is the law of kindness.

She looketh well to the ways of her household, and eateth not the bread of idleness.

Her children arise up, and call her blessed; her husband also, and he praiseth her.

Many daughters have done virtuously, but thou excellest them all.

Favour is deceitful, and beauty is vain: but a woman that feareth the Lord, she shall be praised.

Give her of the fruit of her hands; and let her own works praise her in the gates.

AT THE FUNERAL OF ONE IN PUBLIC LIFE

Ecclesiasticus 44:1-8, 10, 11, 14, 15

LET us now praise famous men, and our fathers that begat us. The Lord hath wrought great glory by them through his great power from the beginning. Such as did bear rule in their kingdoms, men renowned for their power, giving counsel by their understanding, and declaring prophecies: leaders of the people by their counsels, and by their knowledge of learning meet for the people, wise and eloquent in their instructions: such as found out musical tunes, and recited verses in writing: rich men furnished with ability, living peaceably in their habitations: all these were honoured in their generations, and were the glory of their times. There be of them, that have left a name behind them, that their praises might be reported. But these were merciful men, whose righteousness hath not been forgotten. With their seed shall continually remain a good inheritance, and their children are within the covenant. Their bodies are buried in peace; but their name liveth for evermore. The people will tell of their wisdom, and the congregation will shew forth their praise.

AT THE FUNERAL OF A CHILD

II Samuel 12:16-23

DAVID therefore besought God for the child; and David fasted, and went in, and lay all night upon the earth. And the elders of his house arose, and went to him, to raise him up from the earth: but he would not, neither did he eat bread with them. And it came to pass on the seventh day, that the child died. And the servants of David feared to tell him that the child was dead: for they said, Behold, while the child was yet alive, we spake unto him, and he would not hearken unto our voice: how will he then vex himself, if we tell him that the child is dead? But when David saw that his servants whispered, David perceived that the child was dead: therefore David said unto his servants, Is the child dead? And they said, He is dead. Then David arose from the earth, and washed, and anointed himself, and changed his apparel, and came into the house of the Lord, and worshipped: then he came to his own house; and when he required, they set bread before him, and he did eat. Then said his servants unto him, What thing is this that thou hast done? thou didst fast and weep for the child, while it was alive; but when the child was dead, thou didst rise and eat bread. And he said, While the child was yet alive, I fasted and wept: for I said, Who can tell whether God will be gracious to me, that the child may live? But now he is dead, wherefore should I fast? can I bring him back again? I shall go to him, but he shall not return to me.

AT THE FUNERAL OF AN AGED PERSON

Job 5:17-26

BEHOLD, happy is the man whom God correcteth: therefore despise not thou the chastening of the Almighty:

For he maketh sore, and bindeth up: he woundeth, and his hands make whole.

He shall deliver thee in six troubles: yea, in seven there shall no evil touch thee.

In famine he shall redeem thee from death: and in war from the power of the sword.

Thou shalt be hid from the scourge of the tongue: neither shalt thou be afraid of destruction when it cometh.

At destruction and famine thou shalt laugh: neither shalt thou be afraid of the beasts of the earth.

For thou shalt be in league with the stones of the field: and the beasts of the field shall be at peace with thee.

And thou shalt know that thy tabernacle shall be in peace; and thou shalt visit thy habitation, and shalt not sin.

Thou shalt know also that thy seed shall be great, and thine offspring as the grass of the earth.

Thou shalt come to thy grave in a full age, like as a shock of corn cometh in in his season.

Psalm 91

HE that dwelleth in the secret place of the Most High shall abide under the shadow of the Almighty.

I will say of the Lord, He is my refuge

and my fortress: my God, in him will I trust.

Surely he shall deliver thee from the snare of the fowler, and from the noisome pestilence.

He shall cover thee with his feathers, and under his wings shalt thou trust: his truth shall be thy shield and buckler.

Thou shalt not be afraid for the terror by night; nor for the arrow that flieth by day;

Nor for the pestilence that walketh in darkness; nor for the destruction that wasteth at noonday.

A thousand shall fall at thy side, and ten thousand at thy right hand; but it shall not come nigh thee.

Only with thine eyes shalt thou behold and see the reward of the wicked.

Because thou hast made the Lord, which is my refuge, even the most High, thy habitation;

There shall no evil befall thee, neither shall any plague come nigh thy dwelling.

For he shall give his angels charge over thee, to keep thee in all thy ways.

They shall bear thee up in their hands, lest thou dash thy foot against a stone.

Thou shalt tread upon the lion and adder: the young lion and the dragon shalt thou trample under feet.

Because he hath set his love upon me, therefore will I deliver him: I will set him on high, because he hath known my name.

He shall call upon me, and I will answer him: I will be with him in trouble; I will deliver him, and honour him.

With long life will I satisfy him, and shew him my salvation.

READINGS FROM THE
NEW TESTAMENT

St. Matthew 5:3-11

B LESSED are the poor in spirit: for theirs is the kingdom of heaven.

Blessed are they that mourn: for they shall be comforted.

Blessed are the meek: for they shall inherit the earth.

Blessed are they which do hunger and thirst after righteousness: for they shall be filled.

Blessed are the merciful: for they shall obtain mercy.

Blessed are the pure in heart: for they shall see God.

Blessed are the peacemakers: for they shall be called the children of God.

Blessed are they which are persecuted for righteousness' sake: for theirs is the kingdom of heaven.

Blessed are ye, when men shall revile you, and persecute you, and shall say all manner of evil against you falsely, for my sake.

St. John 5:19-29

THEN answered Jesus and said unto them, Verily, verily, I say unto you, The Son can do nothing of himself, but what he seeth the Father do: for what things soever he doeth, these also doeth the Son likewise. For the Father loveth the Son, and sheweth him all things that himself doeth: and he will shew him greater works than these, that ye may marvel. For as the Father raiseth up the dead, and quickeneth them; even so the Son quickeneth whom he will. For the Father judgeth no man, but hath committed all judgment unto the Son: that all men should honour the Son, even as they honour the Father. He that honoureth not the Son honoureth not the Father which hath sent him. Verily, verily, I say unto you, He that heareth my word, and believeth on him that sent me, hath everlasting life, and shall not come into condemnation; but is passed from death unto life. Verily, verily, I say unto you, The hour is coming, and now is, when the dead shall hear the voice of the Son of God: and they that hear shall live. For as the Father hath life in himself; so hath he given to the Son to have life in himself; and hath given him authority to execute judgment also, because he is the Son of man. Marvel not at this: for the hour is coming, in the which all that are in the graves shall hear his voice, and shall come forth; they that have done good, unto the resurrection of life; and they that have done evil, unto the resurrection of damnation.

St. John 11:21-27

THEN said Martha unto Jesus, Lord, if thou hadst been here, my brother had not died. But I know, that even now, whatsoever thou wilt ask of God, God will give it thee. Jesus saith unto her, Thy brother shall rise again. Martha saith unto him, I know that he shall rise again in the resurrection at the last day. Jesus said unto her, I am the resurrection, and the life: he that believeth in me, though he were dead, yet shall he live: and whosoever liveth and believeth in me shall never die. Believest thou this? She saith unto him, Yea, Lord: I believe that thou art the Christ, the Son of God, which should come into the world.

I Peter 1:3-9

Blessed be the God and Father of our Lord Jesus Christ, which according to his abundant mercy hath begotten us again unto a lively hope by the resurrection of Jesus Christ from the dead, to an inheritance incorruptible, and undefiled, and that fadeth not away, reserved in heaven for you, who are kept by the power of God through faith unto salvation ready to be revealed in the last time. Wherein ye greatly rejoice, though now for a season, if need be, ye are in heaviness through manifold temptations: that the trial of your faith, being much more precious than of gold that perisheth, though it be tried with fire, might be found unto praise and honour and glory at the appearing of Jesus Christ: whom having not seen, ye love; in whom, though now ye see him not, yet believing, ye rejoice with joy unspeakable and full of glory: receiving the end of your faith, even the salvation of your souls.

Revelation 7:9-17

After this I beheld, and, lo, a great multitude, which no man could number, of all nations, and kindreds, and people, and tongues, stood before the throne, and before the Lamb, clothed with white robes, and palms in their hands; and cried with a loud voice, saying, Salvation to our God which sitteth upon the throne, and unto the Lamb. And all the angels stood round about the throne, and about the elders and the four beasts, and fell before the throne on their faces, and worshipped God, saying, Amen: Blessing, and glory, and wisdom, and thanksgiving, and honour, and power, and might, be unto our God for ever and ever. Amen. And one of the elders answered, saying unto me, What are these which are arrayed in white robes? and whence came they? And I said unto him, Sir, thou knowest. And he said to me, These are they which came out of great tribulation, and have washed their robes, and made them white in the blood of the Lamb. Therefore are they before the throne of God, and serve him day and night in his temple: and he that sitteth on the throne shall dwell among them. They shall hunger no more, neither thirst any more; neither shall the sun light on them, nor any heat. For the Lamb which is in the midst of the throne shall feed them, and shall lead them unto living fountains of waters: and God shall wipe away all tears from their eyes.

AT THE FUNERAL OF A YOUTH

St. Luke 7:11-16

A ND it came to pass the day after, that he went into a city called Nain; and many of his disciples went with him, and much people. Now when he came nigh to the gate of the city, behold, there was a dead man carried out, the only son of his mother, and she was a widow: and much people of the city was with her. And when the Lord saw her, he had compassion on her, and said unto her, Weep not. And he came and touched the bier: and they that bare him stood still. And he said, Young man, I say unto thee, Arise. And he that was dead sat up, and began to speak. And he delivered him to his mother. And there came a fear on all: and they glorified God, saying, That a great prophet is risen up among us; and, That God hath visited his people.

St. Mark 5:22, 23, 35-42

A ND, behold, there cometh one of the rulers of the synagogue, Jairus by name; and when he saw him, he fell at his feet, and besought him greatly, saying, My little daughter lieth at the point of death: I pray thee, come and lay thy hands on her, that she may be healed; and she shall live. While he yet spake, there came from the ruler of the synagogue's house certain which said, Thy daughter is dead: why troublest thou the Master any further? As soon as Jesus heard the word that was spoken, he saith unto the ruler of the synagogue, Be not afraid, only believe. And he suffered no man to follow him, save Peter, and James, and John the brother of James. And he cometh to the house of the ruler of the synagogue, and seeth the tumult, and them that wept and wailed greatly. And when he was come in, he saith unto them, Why make ye this ado, and weep? the damsel is not dead, but sleepeth. And they laughed him to scorn. But when he had put them all out, he taketh the father and the mother of the damsel, and them that were with him, and entereth in where the damsel was lying. And he took the damsel by the hand, and said unto her, Talitha cumi; which is, being interpreted, Damsel, I say unto thee, arise. And straightway the damsel arose, and walked; for she was of the age of twelve years. And they were astonished with a great astonishment.

PRAYERS

O GOD of lovingkindness and tender mercies, from the deeps of our souls we thank thee for these experiences that call us closer to thee. Through our tears we envision the far reaches of thy providence. We praise thee that when in the ordering of life our earthly body is worn and broken by time and disease, and no longer a fit dwelling place for our immortal spirits, thou dost not keep us in this prison of clay. The hands that were bruised for our transgressions unlatch the door and set the spirit free. Enable us in every hour of sorrow to rejoice in thee for the open door which sometimes we call death. Open wide the gates, O Lord, and receive the spirit of our departed friend into thy everlasting habitations. Grant, we beseech thee, that *he* who has borne the image of the earthly may now bear the image of the heavenly. In fatherly mercy, grant *him* in a better world than this, fullness of life and joy through Jesus Christ our Lord, who broke the bonds of death and liveth for evermore. *Amen.*

—COSTEN J. HARRELL

ALMIGHTY God, our Father, thou hast within thy power and keeping life and death. In thee we find the strength of today and the secret of the day beyond. In thee we have faith for the darkness, and the promise of the cloudless morn. We do not grope in dusty death for life's deepest meanings; we lift our eyes to behold the Resurrection and the Life in Jesus Christ our Lord. We give thee hearty thanks for the beloved one in our circle of love who now lives in thy clearer presence. Let the peace of thy Spirit bring to us the assurance of thy lovingkindness. Let the insight of a triumphant hope possess our hearts.

Thou hast given us the comforting conviction that neither death nor life, nor any other creature, shall be able to separate us from thy love which is in Jesus Christ our Lord. Enable us, we pray thee, to cast all our care upon thee who carest for us. Comfort thou, comfort thou thy people, O God! Speak thou comfortably to the needs of those who feel and know most intimately the meaning of this bereavement.

O God, our Father, lift thou up the light of thy countenance upon us. Turn us again, Lord God of Hosts, and cause thy face to shine upon us, and so our sorrow shall be turned into prayer. For as is thy majesty, so also is thy mercy. In thy will is our peace. May this faith abide in our hearts and grow, until the wounds of parting are healed in the assurance of reunion.

Now, O Lord, lettest thou thy servants depart in peace, according to thy Word, for our eyes have seen thy salvation. Comfort and sustain us by thy companioning mercy, O Shepherd of thy people, and establish us by the still waters and within the pastures of thine all-sufficient grace. Through Jesus Christ our Lord. *Amen.*

—Oscar T. Olson

FOR COMFORT

O LORD Jesus Christ, we beseech thee to comfort these thy servants in their present sorrow; and as thou didst send the Holy Ghost to be the Comforter of thy people, strengthen them by the manifestation of his gracious indwelling, that they may be enabled to contemplate the joy of that better home, where thou art ever seen and worshiped as the light and satisfaction of thine elect, who dwellest with the Father, in the unity of the same Spirit, one God, world without end. *Amen.*

O THOU, who art the God of all comfort, who healest the broken in heart and bindest up their wounds; Mercifully look upon those who are at this time bereaved. Be near them in their sorrow, and let their sorrow draw them nearer unto thee. Now that earthly joys and comfort fail, may the things unseen and eternal grow more real, more present, more full of meaning and power. Let thy strength sustain their weakness; thy grace free their sorrow from bitterness; and thy peace fill their minds with perfect trust in thee; through Jesus Christ our Saviour. *Amen.*

IN THANKSGIVING FOR THE DEAD

WE thank thee, O Lord, for the dear and faithful dead, for those who have made the distant heavens a home for us, and whose truth and beauty are even now in our hearts. One by one thou dost gather the scattered families out of the earthly life into the heavenly glory, from the distractions and strife and weariness of time to the peace of eternity. We thank thee for the labours and joys of these mortal years. We thank thee for the deep sense of the mysteries that lie beyond our dust, and for the eye of faith, which thou hast opened for all who believe in thy Son, to outlook that mark. May we live altogether in thy faith and love, and in that hope which is full of immortality; through the same Jesus Christ our Saviour. *Amen.*

ALMIGHTY God, we offer unto thee most high praise and hearty thanks for the wonderful grace and virtue which thou hast manifested in all thy saints, and in all other holy persons upon earth, who by their lives and labours have shone forth as lights in the several generations of the world; such as were the holy prophets, apostles, and martyrs, whom we remember with honour and commemorate with joy; and for whom, as also for all other thy happy servants, our fathers and brethren, who have departed this life with the seal of faith, we praise and magnify thy holy Name; most humbly desiring that we may still continue in that holy communion, and enjoy the comfort thereof, following, with a glad will and mind, their holy examples of godly living and stedfastness in thy faith; through Jesus Christ our Lord. *Amen.*

O GOD, who dost bring thy children out of darkness and the shadow of death, we thank thee for this departed one in whose love we were blessed, by whose wisdom we were guided, and in whose tenderness we were healed. May the sureness of *his* nearness to us banish loneliness and the sureness of *his* nearness to thee quiet our anxious spirits. In his Name who is our life and light. *Amen.*[1]

—GAIUS GLENN ATKINS

FOR GRACE TO IMITATE A TRIUMPHANT SOUL

O FATHER, Almighty, all merciful, all-loving, suffer us not to miss the glory of this hour through yielding to an overwhelming sense of bereavement. Give us eyes to see and hearts to feel the undefeated courage, the invincible faith, the unconquerable love which thou hast revealed to us in this triumphant soul, who has now passed to the reward of those who unfeignedly love thee. Fill our hearts with praise and gratitude for *his* unshaken conviction that no distress, suffering, or perplexity, neither death, nor things present nor things to come,

[1] Adapted from *The Fellowship of Prayer, 1941.* Used by permission of The Commission on Evangelism and Devotional Life of The Congregational Christian Churches.

could separate us from the love of God which *he* had seen in Christ Jesus our Lord. Let the light which we beheld in *him* never forsake us. And grant to us *his* faith, *his* courage, *his* hope in any trial which may come to us. Bless us with an ever-abiding sense of *his* presence; and we fervently pray that in us *he* may yet behold the fruitage of the travail of *his* body and soul, and be most gloriously satisfied. And this we ask in the Name of *his* Saviour and our Saviour, Jesus Christ our Lord. *Amen.*

FOR A FRIEND

O GOD, the God of the spirits of all flesh, in whose embrace all creatures live, in whatsoever world or condition they be; I beseech thee for *him* whose name and dwelling place and every need thou knowest. Lord, vouchsafe *him* light and rest, peace and refreshment, joy and consolation, in Paradise, in the companionship of saints, in the presence of Christ, in the ample folds of thy great love.

Grant that *his* life (so troubled here) may unfold in thy sight, and find a sweet employment in the spacious fields of eternity. If *he* hath ever been hurt or maimed by any unhappy word or deed of mine, I pray thee of thy great pity to heal and restore *him*, that *he* may serve thee without hindrance.

Tell *him*, O gracious Lord, if it may be, how much I love and miss *him*, and long to see *him* again; and if there be ways in which *he* may come, vouchsafe *him* to me as guide and guard, and grant me a sense of *his* nearness in such degree as thy laws permit.

If in aught I can minister to *his* peace, be pleased of thy love to let this be; and mercifully keep me from every act which may deprive me of the sight of *him* as soon as our trial-time is over, or mar the fulness of our joy when the end of the days hath come.

Pardon, O gracious Lord and Father, whatsoever is amiss in this my prayer, and let thy will be done, for my will is blind and erring, but thine is guided by infinite wisdom, and able to do exceeding abundantly above all that we ask or think; through Jesus Christ our Lord. *Amen.*[2]

--W. GRIFFITHS

[2] Often attributed to William E. Gladstone.

AT THE FUNERAL OF ONE WHO DIED FOR
HIS COUNTRY

ALMIGHTY and most merciful Lord, who didst declare that greater love hath no man than to lay down his life for his friends; hear us, we pray thee, for this our friend, who gave *his* life in service for home and native land. Grant that *his* patriotism and unselfish devotion may make us cherish more deeply that freedom for which our nation stands. May *his* sacrifice not have been made in vain. Give grace, mercy, and peace, we pray thee, to this our comrade and to all men who fight a good fight for righteousness. Through Jesus Christ our Saviour. *Amen.*

—N. B. H., Jr.

AT THE FUNERAL OF A CHILD

O MERCIFUL Father, whose face the angels of thy little ones do always behold in heaven; Grant us stedfastly to believe that this thy child hath been taken into the safe keeping of thine eternal love; through Jesus Christ our Lord. *Amen.*

ALMIGHTY and merciful Father, who dost grant to children an abundant entrance into thy kingdom; Grant us grace so to conform our lives to their innocency and perfect faith, that at length, united with them, we may stand in thy presence in fulness of joy; through Jesus Christ our Lord. *Amen.*

AT THE FUNERAL OF AN AGED PERSON

O LORD God of our fathers, we bless thee for the holy triumphs of thy saints in every age and among all peoples. We thank thee for the battles fought, the victories won, and achievements gained by those who have ceased from their labors and entered into rest. Thou hast said, "The hoary head is a crown of glory, if it be found in the way of righteousness." We thank thee that so often we have been permitted to see this coronation of goodness in thy servants.

Bless all old people everywhere; some have wandered far in life's pathway and mayhap have forgotten thee. Turn, we pray thee, their trembling steps into the ways of life. The young may die, but the old must. Prepare all hearts for this great change.

O Lord, we beseech thee to bless all these relatives and friends, that in their grief and sorrow at this separation they may still know the goodness of God and rely on his unchanging love. May the lessons and precepts and holy examples of thy servants who have died in the Lord be remembered in the years that are to come.

O God, rejoice the souls of thy servants that none of those that trust in thee may be desolate. We pray in the Name of Jesus Christ our Lord. *Amen.*[3]

—ARTHUR H. DeLONG

[3] Adapted from *The Pastor's Ideal Funeral Book.* Used by permission.

SERVICES AT THE GRAVE

A MODERN SERVICE

When the People are assembled, the Minister shall say,

Eye hath not seen, nor ear heard, neither have entered into the heart of man, the things which God hath prepared for them that love him.

For our light affliction, which is but for a moment, worketh for us a far more exceeding and eternal weight of glory.

For if we believe that Jesus died and rose again, even so them also that are fallen asleep in Jesus will God bring with him.

Then the Minister shall say,

Forasmuch as the spirit of this departed loved one hath returned to God who gave it, we therefore tenderly commit *his* body to the ground, in sure trust and certain hope in the power and love of Christ our Lord; at whose divine call they that be asleep in him shall one day rise to stand with him, and hear with all saints the welcome summons: "Enter ye into your Master's joy." For his is the kingdom, and the power, and the glory, for ever. *Amen.*

Then may be said or sung,

Blessed are the dead which die in the Lord from henceforth: yea, saith the Spirit, that they may rest from their labours; and their works do follow them.

Then may be read a Poem or Hymn, followed by extemporary Prayer, or the following:

Our Heavenly Father, who in thy love art ever near to those who need thee; draw close, we pray thee, to these thy children as they seek that comfort which the world can never give. Grant that the sorrows of earth may fit them better for the peace of heaven; and may the loss and pain of life make thy people more ready for the glory that shall yet be revealed. Give courage and a great trust to these dear ones here as they take up their life again, until at last, reunited with those they love, they may all be accorded an abundant entrance into the kingdom of thy glory. We ask through Jesus Christ our Lord. *Amen.*

—N. B. H., Jr.

Then the Minister may say,

THE grace of the Lord Jesus Christ, and the love of God, and the communion of the Holy Spirit, be with you all. *Amen.*

AT THE BURIAL OF A CHILD [1]

When they are come to the Grave shall be said or sung,

JESUS saith to his disciples, Ye now therefore have sorrow: but I will see you again, and your heart shall rejoice, and your joy no man taketh from you.

While the earth is being cast upon the Body, the Minister shall say,

IN sure and certain hope of the Resurrection to eternal life through our Lord Jesus Christ, we commit the body of this child to the ground. The Lord bless *him* and keep *him*, the Lord make his face to shine upon *him* and be gracious unto *him*, the Lord lift up his countenance upon *him*, and give *him* peace, both now and evermore.

[1] From *The Book of Common Prayer* of the Protestant Episcopal Church.

Then shall be said or sung,

THEREFORE are they before the throne of God, and serve him day and night in his temple: and he that sitteth on the throne shall dwell among them.

They shall hunger no more, neither thirst any more; neither shall the sun light on them, nor any heat.

For the Lamb which is in the midst of the throne shall feed them, and shall lead them unto living fountains of waters: and God shall wipe away all tears from their eyes.

Then shall the Minister say,

The Lord be with you.
Answer. And with thy spirit.

Let us pray.

O GOD, whose most dear Son did take little children into his arms and bless them; Give us grace, we beseech thee, to entrust the soul of this child to thy never-failing care and love, and bring us all to thy heavenly kingdom; through the same thy Son, Jesus Christ our Lord. *Amen.*

ALMIGHTY God, Father of mercies and giver of all comfort; Deal graciously, we pray thee, with all those who mourn, that, casting every care on thee, they may know the consolation of thy love; through Jesus Christ our Lord. *Amen.*

MAY Almighty God, the Father, the Son, and the Holy Ghost, bless you and keep you, now and for evermore. *Amen.*

OTHER PRAYERS AT THE GRAVE

WE commend unto thy hands of mercy, most merciful Father, the soul of this our *brother* departed, beseeching thine infinite goodness to give us grace to live in thy fear and love, and to die in thy favor, that both this our *brother*, and we, may be found acceptable in thy sight, and receive that blessing which thy well-beloved Son shall pronounce to all that love and fear thee, saying, "Come, ye blessed of my Father; inherit the kingdom prepared for you from the foundation of the world." Grant this, merciful Father, for the honor of Jesus Christ our Saviour. *Amen.*

O LORD, the God of mercy, unto whom all live; Vouchsafe, we beseech thee, unto this our loved one, a place of refreshment, rest, and the light of everlasting glory, where the light of thy Presence shineth for evermore. And grant that finally we may be united with *him* in the joy of thine eternal glory; through Jesus Christ our Lord. *Amen.*

ALMIGHTY God, with whom do live the spirits of just men made perfect; We humbly commend the soul of this thy servant, our dear *brother*, into thy hands, as into the hands of a faithful Creator and most merciful Saviour; humbly beseeching thee that *he* may be precious in thy sight. Cleanse *him*, we pray thee from every stain of sin, that *he* may be presented pure and without spot before thee; through Jesus Christ our Lord. *Amen.*

FATHER Almighty, God everlasting, Spirit eternal, we bow before thee, for only thy wisdom can know our need and thy compassion measure our sorrow. We do not ask that we may understand the mysteries of life and death, but we pray that thy light may guide us and thy strength sustain us. In thy keeping we trust the spirit of *him* whose earthly work is now ended. *He* asked of thee life, and thou gavest it *him*, even length of days for ever and ever. *He* asked of thee strength, and, by thy gift, *he* has put off that which is mortal and has put on immortality. *He* walked in shadow, and thou hast called *him* into the light of that day which knows no night. O how great is thy goodness, which thou hast laid up for them that love thee; which thou hast wrought for them that put their trust in thee! Help us also to walk in trust and to go forward without fear, till the path of life shall bring us to life eternal. We ask it because thy love is from everlasting to everlasting, in Christ Jesus our Lord. *Amen.*

ALMIGHTY God, who by the death of thy Son Jesus Christ hast destroyed death; by his rest in the tomb hast sanctified the graves of the saints; and by his glorious resurrection hast brought life and immortality to light so that all who die in him abide in hope as to their bodies, and in joy as to their souls; receive, we beseech thee, our unfeigned thanks for that victory over death and the grave which he has obtained for us and for all who sleep in him; and keep us who are still in the body, in everlasting fellowship with all that wait for thee on earth, and with all that are around thee in heaven, in union with him who is the Resurrection and the Life; who liveth and reigneth with thee and the Holy Ghost, ever one God, world without end. *Amen.*

A LMIGHTY, everliving God, the Source of all being and life, whose mercies are infinite and whose love is unceasing; To thee we commend all souls departed, praying thee to cleanse them from every taint and trace of sin, that, in the communion of thy saints, they may find the joy and peace of a perfect life; through the all-sufficient merits of our only Redeemer, Jesus Christ. *Amen.*

O UR Heavenly Father, we rejoice in the blessed communion of all thy saints, wherein thou givest us also to have a part. We remember before thee all who have departed this life in thy faith and love, and especially those most dear to us. We thank thee for our present fellowship with them, for our common hope, and for the promise of future joy. Let the cloud of witnesses, the innumerable company of those who have gone before and en-

tered into rest, be to us an example of godly
life. And even now may we be refreshed with
their joy, that so with patience we may run the
race that remains before us, looking unto Jesus,
the Author and Finisher of our faith; and finally
obtain an entrance into thine everlasting kingdom, the glorious assembly of the saints, and
with them ever worship and adore thy glorious
Name, world without end. *Amen.*

O ALMIGHTY God, who hast knit together
thine elect in one communion and fellowship, in the mystical body of thy Son Christ
our Lord; Grant us grace so to follow thy
blessed Saints in all virtuous and godly living,
that we may come to those unspeakable joys,
which thou hast prepared for those who unfeignedly love thee; through Jesus Christ our
Lord. *Amen.*

O GOD, eternal and unchangeable, we bless
thee that amid all the shadows that fall on
our earthly way, the doubts that perplex and
the fears that hinder us, we have one steadfast
light ever shining upon our path, even the light
of thy love. Thou watchest over us, and we
are safe; thou guidest us, and we cannot lose the

way. We pray for the spirit of trust and obedience, that we may always yield ourselves to thy
will, and find in thee the true rest of our souls,
the true strength of our life, and the joy that
abideth forever.

Be thou, O God, ever with us, within and
without, to strengthen and guard, to guide and
comfort us, that even unto death we may glorify
thy Name. Not of our worthiness, but of thy
tender mercy have regard to our prayers.
Amen.

PUT far from us, O God, all worry and mis-
giving; that having done our best while it
was day, we may, when the night cometh, commit ourselves, our tasks, and those we love, into
thy holy keeping and accept of thee the gift of
sleep. Through Jesus Christ our Lord. *Amen.*

O GOD, comfort thy children, whose hearts
are now sad and heavy with bereavement;
and grant that they may so love and serve thee
that, together with their loved one, they may
obtain the fullness of thy promises in the world
to come. Through Jesus Christ our Lord.
Amen.

PART III

HYMNS AND POEMS

HYMNS

FOR ALL THE SAINTS

For all the saints, who from their labors rest,
Who thee by faith before the world confessed,
Thy Name, O Jesus, be forever blessed,
   Alleluia! Alleluia!

Thou wast their Rock, their Fortress, and their
     Might;
Thou, Lord, their Captain in the well-fought
     fight;
Thou, in the darkness drear, their one true
     Light.
   Alleluia! Alleluia!

O may thy soldiers, faithful, true, and bold,
Fight as the saints who nobly fought of old,
And win with them the victor's crown of gold.
   Alleluia! Alleluia!

O blest communion, fellowship divine!
We feebly struggle, they in glory shine;
Yet all are one in thee, for all are thine.
   Alleluia! Alleluia!

And when the strife is fierce, the warfare long,
Steals on the ear the distant triumph song,
And hearts are brave again, and arms are strong.
  Alleluia! Alleluia!

The golden evening brightens in the west;
Soon, soon, to faithful warriors comes thy rest;
Sweet is the calm of Paradise the blest.
  Alleluia! Alleluia!
                              —WILLIAM W. How

STILL, STILL WITH THEE

Still, still with thee, when purple morning
    breaketh,
  When the bird waketh, and the shadows flee;
Fairer than morning, lovelier than daylight,
  Dawns the sweet consciousness, I am with
    thee.

Alone with thee, amid the mystic shadows,
  The solemn hush of nature newly born;
Alone with thee in breathless adoration,
  In the calm dew and freshness of the morn.

Still, still with thee! As to each newborn morn-
    ing
  A fresh and solemn splendor still is given,
So does this blessed consciousness, awaking,

Breathe each day nearness unto thee and
  heaven.

When sinks the soul, subdued by toil, to slum-
    ber,
  Its closing eyes look up to thee in prayer;
Sweet the repose beneath thy wings o'ershading,
  But sweeter still, to wake and find thee there.

So shall it be at last, in that bright morning,
    When the soul waketh, and life's shadows
      flee;
O in that hour, fairer than daylight dawning,
  Shall rise the glorious thought, I am with thee.
                    —HARRIET BEECHER STOWE

ROCK OF AGES

Rock of Ages, cleft for me,
Let me hide myself in thee;
Let the water and the blood,
From thy wounded side which flowed,
Be of sin the double cure,
Save from wrath and make me pure.

Could my tears for ever flow,
Could my zeal no languor know,
These for sin could not atone;

Thou must save, and thou alone:
In my hand no price I bring;
Simply to thy cross I cling.

While I draw this fleeting breath,
When my eyes shall close in death,
When I rise to worlds unknown,
And behold thee on thy throne:
Rock of Ages, cleft for me,
Let me hide myself in thee.
—AUGUSTUS M. TOPLADY

ABIDE WITH ME

Abide with me: fast falls the eventide;
The darkness deepens; Lord, with me abide!
When other helpers fail, and comforts flee,
Help of the helpless, O abide with me.

Swift to its close ebbs out life's little day;
Earth's joys grow dim, its glories pass away;
Change and decay in all around I see;
O thou, who changest not, abide with me.

I need thy presence every passing hour;
What but thy grace can foil the tempter's
    power
Who, like thyself, my guide and stay can be?

Through cloud and sunshine, Lord, abide with
  me!

I fear no foe, with thee at hand to bless;
Ills have no weight, and tears no bitterness.
Where is death's sting? where, grave, thy vic-
  tory?
I triumph still, if thou abide with me.

Hold thou thy cross before my closing eyes;
Shine through the gloom and point me to the
  skies;
Heaven's morning breaks, and earth's vain shad-
  ows flee;
In life, in death, O Lord, abide with me.
                              —HENRY F. LYTE

LEAD, KINDLY LIGHT

Lead, kindly Light, amid the encircling gloom,
  Lead thou me on!
The night is dark, and I am far from home;
  Lead thou me on!
Keep thou my feet; I do not ask to see
The distant scene—one step enough for me.

I was not ever thus, nor prayed that thou
  Shouldst lead me on;

I loved to choose and see my path; but now
  Lead thou me on!
I loved the garish day, and, spite of fears,
Pride ruled my will: remember not past years.

So long thy power hath blessed me, sure it still
  Will lead me on,
O'er moor and fen, o'er crag and torrent, till
  The night is gone,
And with the morn those angel faces smile;
Which I have loved long since, and lost awhile!
                              —JOHN HENRY NEWMAN

O LOVE THAT WILT NOT LET ME GO

  O Love that wilt not let me go,
    I rest my weary soul in thee;
  I give thee back the life I owe,
  That in thine ocean depths its flow
    May richer, fuller be.

  O Light that followest all my way,
    I yield my flickering torch to thee;
  My heart restores its borrowed ray,
  That in thy sunshine's blaze its day
    May brighter, fairer be.

O Joy that seekest me through pain,
   I cannot close my heart to thee;
I trace the rainbow through the rain,
And feel the promise is not vain
   That morn shall tearless be.

O Cross that liftest up my head,
   I dare not ask to fly from thee;
I lay in dust life's glory dead,
And from the ground there blossoms red
   Life that shall endless be.
          —GEORGE MATHESON

NEARER, MY GOD, TO THEE

Nearer, my God, to thee
   Nearer to thee!
E'en though it be a cross
   That raiseth me;
Still all my song shall be,
Nearer, my God, to thee,
   Nearer to thee!

Though like the wanderer,
   The sun gone down,
Darkness be over me,
   My rest a stone;

Yet in my dreams I'd be
Nearer, my God, to thee,
    Nearer to thee!

There let the way appear,
    Steps unto heaven;
All that thou sendest me,
    In mercy given;
Angels to beckon me
Nearer, my God, to thee,
    Nearer to thee!

Then, with my waking thoughts
    Bright with thy praise,
Out of my stony griefs
    Bethel I'll raise;
So by my woes to be
Nearer, my God, to thee,
    Nearer to thee!

Or if, on joyful wing
    Cleaving the sky,
Sun, moon, and stars forgot,
    Upwards I fly,
Still all my song shall be,
Nearer, my God, to thee,
    Nearer to thee.

—SARAH F. ADAMS

COME, YE DISCONSOLATE

Come, ye disconsolate, where'er ye languish,
    Come to the mercy seat, fervently kneel;
Here bring your wounded hearts, here tell your
        anguish:
    Earth has no sorrow that heaven cannot heal.

Joy of the desolate, Light of the straying,
    Hope of the penitent, fadeless and pure!
Here speaks the Comforter, tenderly saying,
    "Earth has no sorrow that heaven cannot
        cure."

Here see the Bread of Life; see waters flowing
    Forth from the throne of God, pure from
        above:
Come to the feast of love; come, ever knowing
    Earth has no sorrow but heaven can remove.
                                —THOMAS MOORE
                        Alt, by THOMAS HASTINGS

WHEN ON MY DAY OF LIFE

When on my day of life the night is falling,
    And, in the wind from unsunned spaces
        blown,

I hear far voices out of darkness calling
    My feet to paths unknown;

Thou, who hast made my home of life so pleas-
        ant,
    Leave not its tenant when its walls decay;
O Love Divine, O Helper ever present,
    Be thou my strength and stay.

I have but thee, my Father! let thy Spirit
    Be with me then to comfort and uphold;
No gate of pearl, no branch of palm I merit,
    Nor street of shining gold.

Suffice it if—my good and ill unreckoned,
    And both forgiven through thine abounding
        grace—
I find myself by hands familiar beckoned
    Unto my fitting place—

Some humble door among thy many mansions,
    Some sheltering shade where sin and striving
        cease,
And flows for ever through heaven's green ex-
    pansions
    The river of thy peace.

There, from the music round about me stealing,
  I fain would learn the new and holy song,
And find at last, beneath thy trees of healing,
  The life for which I long.
      —JOHN GREENLEAF WHITTIER

JUST AS I AM

Just as I am, without one plea,
But that thy blood was shed for me,
And that thou bidd'st me come to thee,
O Lamb of God, I come, I come!

Just as I am, and waiting not
To rid my soul of one dark blot,
To thee whose blood can cleanse each spot,
O Lamb of God, I come, I come!

Just as I am, though tossed about
With many a conflict, many a doubt,
Fightings and fears within, without,
O Lamb of God, I come, I come!

Just as I am, poor, wretched, blind;
Sight, riches, healing of the mind—
Yea, all I need, in thee to find,
O Lamb of God, I come, I come!

Just as I am!   Thou wilt receive,
Wilt welcome, pardon, cleanse, relieve;
Because thy promise I believe,
O Lamb of God, I come, I come!

Just as I am!   Thy love unknown
Hath broken every barrier down;
Now, to be thine, yea, thine alone,
O Lamb of God, I come, I come!
                                    —CHARLOTTE ELLIOTT

POEMS

CROSSING THE BAR

Sunset and evening star,
    And one clear call for me!
And may there be no moaning of the bar,
    When I put out to sea,

But such a tide as moving seems asleep,
    Too full for sound and foam,
When that which drew from out the bound-
       less deep
    Turns again home.

Twilight and evening bell,
    And after that the dark!
And may there be no sadness of farewell,
    When I embark;

For tho' from out our bourne of Time and
       Place
    The flood may bear me far,
I hope to see my Pilot face to face
    When I have crossed the bar.
              —ALFRED TENNYSON

REQUIEM

Under the wide and starry sky
Dig the grave and let me lie,
Glad did I live and gladly die,
    And I laid me down with a will.

This be the verse you grave for me:
"Here he lies where he longed to be;
Home is the sailor, home from the sea,
    And the hunter home from the hill."
                    —ROBERT LOUIS STEVENSON

TO A WATERFOWL

Whither, 'midst falling dew,
While glow the heavens with the last steps of
        day,
Far, through their rosy depths, dost thou pursue
    Thy solitary way!

Vainly the fowler's eye
Might mark thy distant flight to do thee wrong,
As, darkly painted on the crimson sky,
    Thy figure floats along.

Seek'st thou the plashy brink
Of weedy lake, or marge of river wide,
Or where the rocking billows rise and sink
    On the chafed ocean side?

    There is a Power whose care
Teaches thy way along that pathless coast—
The desert and illimitable air—
    Lone wandering, but not lost.

    All day thy wings have fanned,
At that far height, the cold thin atmosphere,
Yet stoop not, weary, to the welcome land,
    Though the dark night is near.

    And soon that toil shall end;
Soon shalt thou find a summer home, and rest,
And scream among thy fellows; reeds shall
    bend,
    Soon, o'er thy sheltered nest.

    Thou'rt gone, the abyss of heaven
Hath swallowed up thy form; yet, on my heart
Deeply has sunk the lesson thou hast given,
    And shall not soon depart.

He who, from zone to zone,
Guides through the boundless sky thy certain
flight,
In the long way that I must tread alone
Will lead my steps aright.
—WILLIAM CULLEN BRYANT

From THANATOPSIS

So live, that when thy summons comes to join
The innumerable caravan, that moves
To that mysterious realm, where each shall take
His chamber in the silent halls of death,
Thou go not, like the quarry-slave at night,
Scourged to his dungeon, but, sustained and
soothed
By an unfaltering trust, approach thy grave,
Like one who wraps the drapery of his couch
About him, and lies down to pleasant dreams.
—WILLIAM CULLEN BRYANT

From SNOW-BOUND

Yet Love will dream, and Faith will trust,
(Since He who knows our need is just)
That somehow, somewhere, meet we must.
Alas for him who never sees

The stars shine through his cypress trees!
Who, hopeless, lays his dead away,
Nor looks to see the breaking day
Across the mournful marbles play!
Who hath not learned, in hours of faith,
The truth to flesh and sense unknown,
That Life is ever lord of Death,
And Love can never lose its own!
                    —JOHN GREENLEAF WHITTIER

From **THE ETERNAL GOODNESS**

I see the wrong that round me lies,
    I feel the guilt within;
I hear, with groan and travail-cries,
    The world confess its sin.

Yet, in the maddening maze of things,
    And tossed by storm and flood,
To one fixed trust my spirit clings;
    I know that God is good!

I dimly guess from blessings known
    Of greater out of sight,
And, with the chastened Psalmist, own
    His judgments too are right.

I long for household voices gone,
  For vanished smiles I long,
But God hath led my dear ones on,
  And He can do no wrong.

I know not what the future hath
  Of marvel or surprise,
Assured alone that life and death
  His mercy underlies.

And if my heart and flesh are weak
  To bear an untried pain,
The bruisèd reed He will not break,
  But strengthen and sustain.

And so beside the Silent Sea
  I wait the muffled oar;
No harm from Him can come to me
  On ocean or on shore.

I know not where His islands lift
  Their fronded palms in air;
I only know I cannot drift
  Beyond His love and care.
                    —JOHN GREENLEAF WHITTIER

VESTA

O Christ of God! whose life and death
    Our own have reconciled,
Most quietly, most tenderly
    Take home thy star-named child!

Thy grace is in her patient eyes,
    Thy words are on her tongue;
The very silence round her seems
    As if the angels sung.

Her smile is as a listening child's
    Who hears its mother call;
The lilies of Thy perfect peace
    About her pillow fall.

She leans from out our clinging arms
    To rest herself in Thine;
Alone to Thee, dear Lord, can we
    Our well-beloved resign!

O, less for her than for ourselves
    We bow our heads and pray;
Her setting star, like Bethlehem's,
    To Thee shall point the way!
                —John Greenleaf Whittier

From GONE

We miss her in the place of prayer,
    And by the hearth-fire's light;
We pause beside her door to hear
    Once more her sweet "Good-night!"

There seems a shadow on the day,
    Her smile no longer cheers;
A dimness on the stars of night,
    Like eyes that look through tears.

Alone unto our Father's will
    One thought hath reconciled;
That He whose love exceedeth ours
    Hath taken home his child.

Fold her, O Father! in thine arms,
    And let her henceforth be
A messenger of love between
    Our human hearts and thee.
        —JOHN GREENLEAF WHITTIER

THERE IS NO DEATH

There is no death!   The stars go down
    To rise upon some other shore,
And bright in heaven's jeweled crown
    They shine for evermore.

There is no death!   The forest leaves
  Convert to life the viewless air;
The rocks disorganize to feed
  The hungry moss they bear.

There is no death!   The dust we tread
  Shall change, beneath the summer show-
    ers,
To golden grain, or mellow fruit,
  Or rainbow-tinted flowers.

And ever near us, though unseen,
  The dear immortal spirits tread;
For all the boundless universe
  Is Life—there are no dead! [1]
                    —JOHN L. MCCREERY

THE FATHER'S HOUSE

The Father's house has many rooms,
              And each is fair;
And some are reached through gathered
  glooms
              By silent stair;
But he keeps house, and makes it home,
Whichever way the children come.

[1] Often erroneously ascribed to Bulwer-Lytton.

Plenty and peace are everywhere
      His house within;
The rooms are eloquent with prayer,
      The songs begin;
And dear hearts, filled with love, are glad,
Forgetting that they once were sad.

The Father's house is surely thine,
      Therefore why wait?
His lights of love through darkness shine,
      The hour grows late.
Push back the curtain of thy doubt,
And enter—none will cast thee out!
          —MARIANNE FARNINGHAM

THE WATCHER

She always leaned to watch for us,
    Anxious if we were late,
In winter by the window,
    In summer by the gate;

And though we mocked her tenderly,
    Who had such foolish care,
The long way home would seem more safe
    Because she waited there.

Her thoughts were all so full of us—
    She never could forget!
And so I think that where she is
    She must be watching yet,

Waiting till we come home to her,
    Anxious if we are late—
Watching from heaven's window,
    Leaning from heaven's gate.[2]
                    —MARGARET WIDDEMER

MOTHER

True heart and wise, that with Love's key
Didst open all life's mystery
And buy life's treasure at the price
Of Love's perpetual sacrifice!

The peace that Love finds hid in care;
The strength that love-bourne burdens bear;
The hope that stands with love and faith
Serenely facing life and death!

The blessing that in blessing lies—
These didst thou know, true heart and wise!

[2] From *Cross Currents*, by Margaret Widdemer. Copyright, 1921, by Harcourt, Brace & Co., Inc.

Now God hath added, last and best,
The sudden, glad surprise of rest! [3]
—ROSSITER W. RAYMOND

ON THE DEATH OF AN AGED FRIEND

You are not dead—Life has but set you free!
   Your years of life were like a lovely song,
   The last sweet poignant notes of which, held
      long,
Passed into silence while we listened, we
Who loved you listened still expectantly!
   And we about you whom you moved among
   Would feel that grief for you were surely
      wrong—
You have but passed beyond where we can see.

For us who knew you, dread of age is past!
You took life, tiptoe, to the very last;
   It never lost for you its lovely look;
   You kept your interest in its thrilling book;
To you Death came no conqueror; in the end—
You merely smiled to greet another friend! [4]
—ROSELLE MERCIER MONTGOMERY

[3] Used by permission.
[4] Used by permission.

OTHER BRIEF SELECTIONS

Servant of God, well done!
   Thy glorious warfare's past;
The battle's fought, the race is won,
   And thou art crowned at last.
           —CHARLES WESLEY

He liveth long who liveth well;
   All other life is short and vain;
He liveth longest who can tell
   Of living most for heavenly gain.

He liveth long who liveth well;
   All else is being flung away;
He liveth longest who can tell
   Of true things truly done each day.
           —HORATIOUS BONAR

There is a world above,
   Where parting is unknown;
A whole eternity of love,
   Form'd for the good alone;
And faith beholds the dying here
Translated to that happier sphere.
           —JAMES MONTGOMERY

Servant of God, well done!
  Rest from thy loved employ:
The battle fought, the victory won,
  Enter thy Master's joy.

The pains of death are past,
  Labor and sorrow cease,
And Life's long warfare closed at last,
  Thy soul is found in peace.
                    —JAMES MONTGOMERY

How wonderful is Death,
Death and his brother Sleep!
                    —PERCY B. SHELLEY

. . . . All that is, at all,
  Lasts ever, past recall;
Earth changes, but thy soul and God stand sure:
  What entered into thee,
  That was, is, and shall be:
Time's wheel runs back or stops; Potter and
  clay endure.
                    —ROBERT BROWNING

Harken, harken!
God speaketh in thy soul,
Saying, "O thou that movest

With feeble steps across this earth of mine,
To break beside the fount thy golden bowl
   And spill its purple wine,—
Look up to heaven and see how like a scroll
My right hand hath thine immortality
In an eternal grasping."
      —ELIZABETH B. BROWNING

Thou wilt not leave us in the dust:
   Thou madest man, he knows not why;
   He thinks he was not made to die;
And thou hast made him: thou art just.
      —ALFRED TENNYSON

I hold it true, whate'er befall;
   I feel it, when I sorrow most;
   'Tis better to have loved and lost
Than never to have loved at all.
      —ALFRED TENNYSON

God calls our loved ones, but we lose not
      wholly
   What He hath given;
They live on earth, in thought and deed, as truly
   As in his Heaven.
      —JOHN GREENLEAF WHITTIER

Swing softly, beauteous gates of death,
   To let a waiting soul pass on
Achievement crowns life's purposes
   And victory is forever won.

Swing softly, softly, heavenly gate,
   Thy portal passed, no more to roam;
Our traveler finds her journey o'er
   And rest at last in "Home Sweet Home."
         —ALICE B. HOWE

So on I go not knowing;
   I would not if I might;
I would rather walk in the dark with God
   Than walk alone in the light;
I would rather walk with him by faith,
   Than walk alone by sight.
         —MARY GARDNER BRAINARD

If thou shalt be in heart a child—
Forgiving, tender, meek, and mild—
Though with light stains of earth defiled,
   O soul, it shall be well!
         —WILLIAM MORRIS

APPENDIX

PROFESSIONAL CONDUCT [1]

A minister in charge of a funeral finds himself in one of the most difficult of situations. He represents God, under whose watch-care all events, even death, take place; he represents humanity in its efforts to assuage the bitterness of the hour; and at the same time he represents his own ecclesiastical organization, his own profession, in conducting a public service. The keynote of right conduct in all these various relationships will be found in a calm, assured attitude in both voice and bearing.

PREFUNERAL DUTIES

When death is imminent in a home of his congregation, the pastor should know of it and keep in close touch. He is put in an awkward position if he has been informed that a parishioner is sick and then fails to call before death occurs. A lingering illness will summon the pastor many times; but when the sick person's hours are seen to be numbered, the good pastor arranges to make his visits increasingly frequent. A last "commendatory" prayer is often repeated at the bedside of the dying. This prayer, without harshly resigning the loved one to death,

---

[1] This chapter and portions of the following chapter are a revision and enlargement of the section on the funeral in my *Ministerial Ethics and Etiquette* (Cokesbury Press, 1928).

should trustfully commit him to the love and mercy of the heavenly Father.

When death occurs, the pastor should go to the home at once. Perhaps he has been there a few hours before—it does not matter; he should go back again. His instant presence will mean far more to the family than any number of beautifully delivered Sunday sermons later on. The visit need not be long, but it should include prayer if possible.

Other duties permitting, the pastor should be in and out of the home two or three times between the death and the funeral. The more time he can spend with his people then, the better ministry he can give them. Let him not act professionally—anything but that. If he can make himself one of the home for the time being, helping here and there, talking quietly with visitors and friends, such unobtrusive helpfulness will be the very height of professional service—and that because it appears so unprofessional.

ARRANGEMENTS

A good pastor is sometimes able to help the family in making funeral arrangements. He will of course be consulted about his own part in the service, and thus have opportunity to help agree on a convenient time and to discuss briefly the type of service he plans to hold. If the family sincerely seek his counsel, he can offer, with due caution, his guidance on other matters of taste and judgment. However, for obvious reasons, he should have nothing to do with the selection of an undertaker.

Although in most cases it never enters the minds of the family that anyone but their own pastor shall be in charge of the funeral, it is not good form for him to "offer" his services. Occasionally relatives request that an old friend or former pastor "conduct" the service and that their own pastor assist. Professional ethics demands in such a case that the outside minister tactfully insist on taking the secondary place; he may preach the sermon and otherwise assume an important role, but the home pastor must be "in charge" and open and close the service.

PRAYER WITH THE FAMILY

Some pastors find it a very effective ministry to have a prayer alone with the bereaved family just previous to the public funeral service. Such an occasion gives opportunity for an intimacy in prayer that may be extremely helpful. Furthermore, the minister can so point his prayer as to get the minds of the family prepared for the longer service about to begin. On the other hand, there are times when manifestations of grief and excitement counsel against this.

AT THE CHURCH

If it is planned for the minister to accompany the funeral party to the church, he should see to it that he is at the home several minutes beforehand—not "just at the hour." If he is to meet the party at the church, he should be ready some minutes before the service has been announced to begin—in time, if he is in personal charge of the service, to ascertain that the organist and choir are ready and that everyone who is to take part has a copy of the program. There should be no last-minute bustling about to complete arrangements, and no unnecessary talking or movement which might disturb the atmosphere of quietness and reverence.

When the funeral is to be held in the church, the entrance of the funeral party at the beginning of the service is often a formal processional. The officiating minister meets the body at the door as the pall-bearers bring it up the steps and precedes it down the aisle reading such words as his church may provide, or as he himself selects. When several ministers are present, they march by twos in the processional, and the one who reads goes in front of all. Many object to the formal funeral processional at the beginning of the service as an unnecessary parade of grief, and in certain sections of the country it is seldom seen today in nonliturgical churches. Instead, the body is brought to the church in advance and rests in place before the people arrive. Then at the start of the service the minister simply enters quietly and takes his place.

The funeral service is often held at the house or, more and more frequently in recent years, at the undertaker's chapel. The service itself is much the same, though perhaps somewhat less formal. The undertaker provides a place for the minister to stand, ordinarily near the casket, and arranges other necessary details.

AT THE INTERMENT

At the conclusion of the service in the church, the minister leaves the pulpit and precedes the body in a slow procession up the aisle and out to the hearse. The people quietly stand until the family, following the pallbearers, have left the church. At the house or funeral parlor the procedure is similar, but the minister should consult the undertaker in advance as to which aisle or exit to take. At the hearse he stands while the casket is being put in place. During this time and at the cemetery, it is almost instinctive for men to remove their hats in honor of the dead; but the living ought not to be so jeopardized in bad weather. The minister may say to the pallbearers, "Let us keep on our hats, gentlemen," and set the example. Sometimes the hand may be put to the hat brim as an expression of respect.

In some parts of the country it is common for the service at the grave to accompany actual interment. In such cases, timing of the minister's words with the actions of the undertaker and his assistants is necessary; and consultation in advance is advisable, as the procedure varies according to local custom and the equipment of the undertaker. As soon as all is prepared, the minister begins to read the introductory interment sentences, and simultaneously the casket is lowered into the grave. He must then pause while the lowering apparatus is removed and preparations are made for filling in the earth, after which he reads the statement of committal while the first earth is cast. Sometimes the undertaker or

182 THE PASTOR'S IDEAL FUNERAL MANUAL

some friend drops the petals of a crushed flower rather than actual earth during the phrase "earth to earth, ashes to ashes, dust to dust" when this type of committal is used. Then in some cases the minister waits again until the grave is filled and covered with flowers before concluding the service with prayer and a benediction; in others the handful of earth symbolizes the filling in until after the service.

Of recent years there has been a well-founded objection to having the bereaved witness the process of interment. The sight of the coffin disappearing beneath the surface of the ground is ordinarily most painful to the family and close friends, and not infrequently has resulted in violent manifestations of grief. In many communities interment in the presence of the whole funeral party is now rare; and the minister will do well to promote by tactful advice adoption of this practice elsewhere, particularly when some of the family seem greatly agitated in their grief. In such cases, the casket is prepared to go into the grave but not lowered—at least not enough to disappear from sight. The minister then conducts his entire service without interruption and dismisses the company with the benediction. All disperse except the pallbearers or a few close friends, who remain to witness the interment. Members of the family return alone later if they wish, after the grave has been completed. Ordinarily the minister leaves at the end of his service and does not return. He may, if he judges it advisable, say a word of personal farewell to the family. In any case he should call on the family again within a few hours.

THE SERVICE IN DETAIL

Perfection in all details of the funeral service should be the aim of the minister, and to its planning he should give the utmost care. He should of course ascertain the wishes of the family. Usually they are glad to leave everything to his judgment, expressing a choice only as to music. If a special request is made, he cannot very well refuse it unless a rule of his church or definite religious convictions are involved, but he can often tactfully advise the best procedure. He is in a better position to do this if he has his own plans well in mind and can for the most part present them for approval rather than ask the family for their ideas. He should be sure the members of the family understand and do not object to any proposed departure from the customs of the community. Within these limits and the rules of his church the minister should feel free to adopt whatever service he judges appropriate for the age, sex, and character of the deceased.

USING STANDARD LITURGIES

The three funeral rituals contained in Part I of this Manual are the latest revisions of the traditional services of the respective denominations, and thus incorporate time-tested material, reconsidered, selected, and arranged to conform with modern practice. The minister will often find in one of them all he needs for a given occasion. It should be noted that each provides for a number of alternatives and also suggests points for inserting hymns and a sermon, so that considerable variety in the use of any one service is possible.

SUGGESTED PROGRAMS

When the minister wishes to construct his own service, the first step should be the laying out of a general outline or program. Perhaps the following will be found as suitable as any for the average funeral:

Processional sentences
Invocation
Hymn
Readings from the Old Testament
Readings from the New Testament
Hymn
Sermon, meditation, or reading
Prayer
Benediction

If a service without vocal music is desired, the hymns may be omitted from this order without rearranging other items—similarly the sermon. In fact, any items may be omitted except at least one reading from the Scriptures and a prayer. For example, a brief service might follow this program:

Processional sentences
Short prayer
Readings from the Old Testament

    Readings from the New Testament
    Reading—words of a hymn or a poem
    Prayer
    Benediction

On the other hand, the service may be expanded by adding another hymn between the Old and New Testament readings or after the sermon and by adding a prayer after the scripture readings. If additional ministers take part, even further expansion is possible by having each say or read some words under the sermon heading, interspersing a hymn or prayer if desired. The leading minister as a rule opens the service and pronounces the final prayer and the benediction. The other parts he assigns according to his own judgment.

So far as is practical, the service should be planned to proceed without announcement. An introduction for a second minister is better omitted. If it is considered necessary, it should be brief and matter-of-fact; words of praise for one taking part are quite foreign to the purpose of the service. Careful planning and a copy of the program for each participant will in most cases permit smooth flow with the aid of only an occasional scarcely perceptible sign.

The order given above is merely suggestive, and the minister may wish to outline his program differently. In doing so, however, he should guard against formlessness or conglomeration. There should be a definite progression of the various elements toward a climax, and by the very nature of the funeral service it would seem that this climax ought to be the funeral prayer.

PROCESSIONAL SENTENCES

When the funeral service begins with a processional, the traditional sentences read by the leader are almost a necessity. Even without a processional, such words of scriptural assurance still seem a more impressive beginning than any announcement,— even so simple a phrase as, "Let us pray." They can be chosen from any of the wealth of verses which give assurance of everlasting life, of the mercy and lovingkindness of Almighty God, and of his presence in time of need. The verses of the Old Testament which declare in poetic language the transience of this life are also proper, but should be followed by one or more statements of the immortal life to follow.

THE INVOCATION

A short prayer at the beginning will be proper in most cases, even for a very brief service. As with any invocation, it is a request for God's presence, and is made applicable to the funeral occasion by mention of the special need in time of trouble and sorrow.

SCRIPTURE READINGS

Passages from the Old Testament appropriate for the funeral are: first, those which suggest in noble language the universality of death as the way of all the earth; and, second, those which declare that God is both all-powerful and all-merciful, that he can and will comfort, strengthen, and sustain those who put their trust in him. There is of course no great emphasis on eternal life in the Old Testament. For full expression of this supreme consolation one selects the assuring words of Christ himself, and those inspired by his Spirit as recorded in the New Testament. All three ideas should be expressed in the scripture readings at a funeral, and logic suggests that they come in the order of increasing importance. Since the first two ideas are incomplete without the Christian assurance of the New Testament, the readings from the latter should follow immediately or closely upon those from the Old Testament.

PRAYERS

Nothing in the funeral occasion can be more important than the prayers. Probably every service should include at least one formal prayer whose origin is lost in antiquity. Death and bereavement are universal and move all hearts to the same feeling; it is just as well that those who mourn today should recognize this. Probably also every service, especially for nonliturgical people, should include at least one "extemporary" prayer. Although the mourner needs to realize his oneness with humanity in suffering, he needs too the consoling assurance that his own sorrow is individual and personal to God. Sometimes introducing the name of the deceased in a reference to "our departed brother" will be enough to give the needed personal touch.

THE SERMON

The word "sermon" as used here may cover any original words addressed to the congregation—or even the reading of a poem, the words of a hymn, or a series of suitable quotations with or without explanatory paragraphs connecting. The traditional funeral sermon has largely disappeared; and many funerals today, even in nonliturgical churches, include nothing extemporary except possibly one prayer. Nevertheless, the minister will often find that an appropriate short message or meditation not only is highly acceptable but also adds immeasurably to the continuing ministry of the service. Brief, well-pointed words of comfort and guidance at the funeral of a loved one may sink deeper and remain longer than those of any other sermon.

If a sermon is used, it is always a question how much should be said about the deceased. Unless the minister has known the deceased well and favorably, it usually proves that a few generalities—or silence—are safer. If special remarks seem called for, these may include allusions which make this part of the service something more than a formality; the bereaved may be entitled to some assurance that the life they loved has not been in vain nor passed without personal notice. Where the deceased is a stranger or one whose life was not such as to commend it to favorable public notice, the minister is wise to stick to generalities and leave judgment in the hands of God.

MUSIC

With increasing frequency there is a request that there be "no music." The feeling undoubtedly results from the fact that inappropriate or poorly rendered music can be more agonizing in the hour of grief than at any other time.

Commonly the music at a funeral is the singing of standard hymns. For a large church funeral, the regular choir is not inappropriate; but a full choir might seem to overwhelm a small company. A few voices, such as a quartet, or even a soloist, are generally more desirable. These voices should be well-trained and accustomed to singing together; a hastily assembled group is likely to produce a poorly balanced ensemble, if not embarrassing errors.

Within recent years, there has come about the practice of having soft organ music played before and after the service. Ordinarily instrumental music is more soothing than vocal. When singing is not desired, reading the words of a hymn can effectively serve instead.

On page 193 is a list of hymns frequently used at funerals. All of them cannot be recommended: for the tunes of some are not in the proper atmosphere, and the words of some imply theological ideas not widely approved today. But when a certain song has dear associations for those who mourn, its use in the hour of sorrow may be very comforting—even more so than the unfamiliar sound of one which by all other counts is far superior.

THE BENEDICTION

It is quite common for the funeral service to end without a benediction, an announcement being made such as, "The service will be continued at the cemetery." This is not inappropriate if all present will follow the casket to the graveside. However, often today many of those attending the service at the church leave without joining the procession to the cemetery. When this dispersal is to be expected, it is more impressive and more fitting to let the people depart with the blessing of a benediction. Practically any of the usual benedictions is appropriate for the funeral.

THE SERVICE AT THE GRAVE

The service at the grave in most instances should be quite brief. It is not helpful to the bereaved to make the painful final farewell lingering. An exception may occur when the burial takes place at a distance from the preceding church service, as there is almost an entirely different company present. When the weather is inclement, one should remember that grief has physical effects, and that the service may properly be reduced to a minimum without implying disrespect. Usually the traditional order of introductory sentences, committal, and prayer is sufficient. Sometimes a hymn or poem may be read before the final prayer or benediction. Music at the grave, because of the difficulty of accompaniment, is unusual though not at all unknown.

The introductory sentences in the original Eng-

lish Prayer Book—preserved as the first series in
the Protestant Episcopal liturgy—consisted of Job
14:1-2 followed by a medieval antiphon, and were
known as "anthems" because often sung or chanted.
Today most ministers prefer the use of Scripture
alone. Both as an impressive opening to this part of
the service, and as a final opportunity to give comfort by the assurance of the Scriptures, these scriptural sentences may well be included.

The traditional committal—to which the third
form in the Methodist liturgy is most similar in this
book—has long been a theological battlefield. More
recently it has been objected to on account of the
phrase "earth to earth, ashes to ashes, dust to dust,"
which many consider harsh and unnecessary. The
phrase may be omitted from any of the older forms,
if desired; or, as is the case with many ministers
today, one of the more modern committals may be
used. These emphasize the spirit rather than the
body.

In special instances where the body is not to be
left to rest in the earth, any of the modern committals can be altered to fit the circumstances by
substituting for the phrase "to the ground," as fol-
lows:

    Mausoleum—"to its resting place"

    At sea—"to the deep"

    Cremation—"to the elements"

The committal is traditionally followed by another "anthem," Revelation 14:13, if it can be rea-
sonably assumed that the deceased did "die in the
Lord."

Prayers at the grave do not differ greatly from those at the church except that they may take into account the leavetaking implied in the committal. They may commend the spirit of the deceased to God's love, express gratitude for the assurance of immortality, petition on behalf of the living, grace to continue in righteousness and at length be joined again in the life to come, and express other appropriate sentiments. The service is of course concluded with the final benediction.

FUNERAL HYMN LIST

* Abide with me—Henry F. Lyte.
   Asleep in Jesus!—Margaret Mackay.
   Beautiful River—Robert Lowry.
   Beautiful valley of Eden—Walter O. Cushing.
* Come, ye disconsolate—Thomas Moore.
   Face to face—Mrs. Frank A. Breck.
   Fade, fade each earthly joy—Jane C. Bonar.
* For all the saints—William W. How.
   Forever with the Lord—James Montgomery.
   Gathering Home—Mariana B. Slade.
   Hark, hark my soul!—Frederick W. Faber.
   He leadeth me: O blessed thought!—Joseph H. Gilmore.
   I know that my Redeemer lives—Charles Wesley.
   I need thee every hour—Annie S. Hawks.
   I will sing you a song—Ellen H. Gates.
   It singeth low in every heart—John W. Chadwick.
   Jerusalem the golden—Bernard of Cluny.
   Jesus, Lover of my soul—Charles Wesley.
* Just as I am—Charlotte Elliott.
   Jesus, Saviour, pilot me—Edward Hopper.
* Lead, kindly Light—John Henry Newman.
   My faith looks up to thee—Ray Palmer.

* The words of the hymns preceded by an asterisk are reproduced in Part III of this book.

My heavenly home is bright and fair—William Hunter

My Jesus, as thou wilt—Benjamin Schmolck.

* Nearer, my God, to thee—Sarah F. Adams.

Not Half Has Ever Been Told—John Burch Atchinson.

Now the laborer's task is o'er—John Ellerton.

O God, our help in ages past—Isaac Watts.

* O Love that wilt not let me go—George Matheson.

One sweetly solemn thought—Phoebe Cary.

* Rock of Ages—Augustus M. Toplady.

Safe in the arms of Jesus—Fanny J. Crosby.

Saved by Grace—Fanny J. Crosby.

Servant of God, well done—Charles Wesley.

Shall we meet beyond the river?—H. L. Hastings.

* Still, still with thee—Harriet Beecher Stowe.

Sweet By and By—S. F. Bennett.

Ten thousand times ten thousand—Henry Alford.

The Home Over There—D. W. C. Huntington.

The Homeland, O the Homeland—Hugh R. Haweis.

The Unclouded Day—J. K. Alwood.

There is a land of pure delight—Isaac Watts.

What a Friend we have in Jesus—Joseph Scriven.

When my life-work is ended—Fanny J. Crosby.

* When on my day of life—John Greenleaf Whittier.

IDEAS FOR SERMONS [1]

SOLACE FOR TROUBLED HEARTS

Let not your heart be troubled: ye believe in God, believe also in me.—John 14:1.

1. Man a creature of sorrow and trouble; man's peculiar heritage—Ps. 90:10; Job 5:7; 14:1.
2. Man's sad heritage of sorrow not hopeless.
   a) It argues superior capacities and endowments of soul life.
   b) It argues that an all-wise and all-loving Creator should provide some solace or cordial for sorrow—Isa. 51:12.
3. Jesus, God's chosen Agent to present this only true solace to the world—Isa. 61:1-2; Luke 4:16-21. He offers heaven's remedy freely to all: his love, sacrifice, sympathy, healing, and help—Luke 7:11-15; John 11:33-44; Matt. 11:28-29.
4. Of all sorrows and troubles, none so distracting and despairing as those caused by death. Jesus was facing death and his disciples despair. Soon he would be on the cross and his disciples scattered; hence he says, "Let not. . ."—John 16:6, 22.
5. Faith in God and Jesus Christ his Son is the solace for troubled hearts. God, Christ, heaven are the great words at such a time.

—Edward Baech

[1] Adapted from *The Pastor's Ideal Funeral Book* by Arthur H. DeLong.

COMFORT ALL THAT MOURN

To comfort all that mourn.—Isa. 61:2.

1. Mourning for the dead is common to all the race of mankind; began with mother Eve; has continued through all ages and among all peoples. Never get used to the sorrow and separation caused by death—Gen. 37:35; Jer. 31:15.

2. We should thank God for the power to love and to mourn. Not like brute beasts; man is godlike in love, sorrow, and all soul life. Shows all the finer qualities of the soul—John 11:31, 35.

3. Special mission of Jesus, as announced by himself was "to heal the broken-hearted"—Luke 4:18—and "comfort all that mourn"—Isa. 61:2; Matt. 5:4. Definition of word "comfort." Jesus cares. He is the Great Comforter—John 14:1-2. Other comforters: friends—John 11:31; Holy Spirit—John 14:16.

4. He comforts with hopes of future life, and meeting our loved ones there—John 11:25; Matt. 5:4.

—A. H. D.

DEATH AND JUDGMENT

It is appointed unto men once to die, but after this the judgment.—Heb. 9:27.

1. Two solemn events in the history of all; both are inevitable—Eccles. 3:20; II Cor. 5:10. Death God's call to judgment—Rev. 20:12.

2. The great assize—Acts 17:31. All called—Rom. 2:3. None excused—Rom. 14:12. No escape—

Rom. 2:3; Amos 9:1-4; Ps. 139:7-12. High and low—Luke 1:52. Oppressed and oppressor—Ps. 72:4. Saint and sinner—Eccles. 3:17; Rom. 2:2-16.

3. The Judge, the Lord Jesus—Matt. 25:31. His majesty and glory—Dan. 7:9-10; Rev. 6:15-16. Mercy has made her plea; Justice now takes the throne—Ps. 89:14; Prov. 1:24-31; Ps. 97:2.

4. Books opened—Rev. 20:12. Book of law—Deut. 30:10; Gal. 3:10. Conscience—Rom. 1:19, 28-32. Memory—Mal. 3:16. Works—Eccles. 12:14; Ezek. 7:3; I Cor. 4:5; Rev. 14:13. Life—Rev. 20:15; Luke 10:20; Dan. 12:1.

5. The final sentence—Matt. 25:21, 34, 41, 46; Rom. 2:5-9; Rev. 14:13.

—A. H. D.

THE EARTHLY TENT AND THE HEAVENLY HOUSE

For we know that if our earthly house of this tabernacle were dissolved, we have a building of God, an house not made with hands, eternal in the heavens.—II Cor. 5:1.

1. Paul the champion preacher of the resurrection. His Epistles full of argument and illustration—I Cor. 15, etc.; I Thess. 4:13-18. Text draws striking contrasts: "earthly tabernacle"—"eternal house."

2. The earthly house, the body:
   a) Distinct from its tenant, the soul—II Cor. 5:6.

The body decays—II Cor. 4:16.   The soul
endures—II Cor. 4:17-18.

b) Cannot stand the storm and stress of life; dis-
solves; weatherbeaten tent.   And is this *all?*

3. The house of God; what beyond?   I have a right
to know—I Cor. 15:19; I Thess. 4:13.   "We
know"—text.

a) A spiritual body—I Cor. 15:44.

b) Glorified and like Christ's—Phil. 3:21; I Cor.
15:43.

c) Eternal—II Cor. 4:18; Heb. 12:27-28.

d) In the heavens—Heb. 11:14-16; 12:22; Rev.
21:10-27.

—A. H. D.

SUFFER THEM TO COME

*But Jesus said, Suffer little children, and forbid
them not, to come unto me: for of such is the kingdom of heaven.*—Matt. 19:14.

1. It is a divine command from a loving Lord.   He
knows what is best for them and us.   Jesus loved
the little ones.   He exalted, dignified, and by
his incarnation deified babyhood.   Infants were
thought but little of before Christ came.   He rebuked his disciples for their indifference—Matt.
19:14; 18:6.   There is a peculiar sadness in the
death of children.   Their going breaks many
cords.

2. But there is a bright side.   Dying children go to
Christ and heaven.

a) They are saved from cares and sorrows of life—Mark 10:14-15.
b) They never taste the pangs of personal sin—Matt. 18:10, 14.
c) Their salvation is forever secure—Matt. 18:10.
d) Parents should be submissive to the divine will—Job 1:21; II Kings 4:26; II Sam. 12:23.
                                                —JOHN A. DIEKMAN

A LITTLE CHILD SHALL LEAD THEM

And a little child shall lead them.—Isa. 11:6.

1. The influence of a little child. Who can tell its power: in the life, in the home, etc.? Tiny hands touch tender cords, rebuke discords and produce harmonies. God's evangels to us. Their ministries should be wholesome, helpful, and saving.
2. Why, then, does God take them from us? Better ask why he gives them to us. They have been with us and fulfilled their mission here. Better to love and lose than not to love at all. Develops tenderness, love, and sympathy. God gives more than he takes—Job 1:21.
3. Our dead children may lead us to him and to heaven.
   a) We know *they* are in heaven—Matt. 18:10; 19:14.
   b) Where our love centers, there we want to go—Matt. 6:21.
   c) What they could not do in life they may do in death.
                                                —A. H. D.

BE READY

Be ye also ready: for in such an hour as ye think not the Son of man cometh.—Matt. 24:44.

1. Death in youth seems unnatural. Nature has her seasons: seedtime and harvest, bud and bloom, blossom and fruitage, opening bud and falling leaf, summer and winter. Not so death.
2. Death has all seasons. Infant of days, man of years, youth and maiden, man and woman; no sex is spared, no age exempt.
3. The time of death is unknown, day and hour—Matt. 25:13. A wise provision. Foreknowledge is withheld but memory given; why? Life happier, activities more intense, plans bigger and better than if we knew.
4. But uncertainty urges readiness. Youth the time for joy. Yes, but readiness for death should only increase the joy of life—Ps. 90:14; Eccles. 11:9.
5. What is necessary to "be ready"?
   a) Faith in Christ—John 3:3, 14-15.
   b) Knowledge of sins forgiven—Rev. 21:27.
   c) Doing the will of God—Matt. 24:42-51; 25:31-46.

—A. H. D.

RIPE FOR HARVESTING

Thou shalt come to thy grave in a full age, like as a shock of corn cometh in his season.—Job 5:26.

1. God's last and best promise to a good man. Beautiful symbolism in vss. 17-26, fulfilled in Job

42:17. Death seems natural and no calamity in such cases. Abraham—Gen. 25:8; David— I Chron. 29:28. God both sower and gleaner, our Friend—Job 1:21.

2. Seed sown. Life opportunity. Character. No seedtime, no harvest—Eccles. 11:4-6. Have a care what kind of seed—Gal. 6:7-8; Prov. 22:8; 11:18; Hos. 10:12; I Pet. 1:23; John 3:7.

3. The growth. Good soil—Matt. 13:8. Cultivation—Matt. 13:19. Growth gradual—Mark 4:28; but vigorous—Ps. 92:12-14; Eph. 4:15; II Pet. 3:18.

4. The fruit, a holy life. Fruits of Spirit—Gal. 5:22-23. Good deeds—Matt. 25:34-40; Acts 11:24. Good name—Prov. 22:1; Eccles. 7:1.

5. The harvest home, a time not for tears, but for joy—Isa. 9:3. The soul full, ripe by the Sun of Righteousness—Mal. 4:2. Profitable for husbandman, earth, heaven, the glorified soul—Isa. 35:10; Exod. 34:22; Rev. 14:15.

—A. H. D.

SUGGESTIVE THEMES AND TEXTS

COMFORT

A Comforting Invitation—Matt. 11:28; Ps. 101:2; Rev. 22:17.

A Father of the Fatherless—Ps. 68:5, 146:9; Jer. 49:11.

Affliction, Momentary; Glory, Eternal—II Cor. 4:17.

Another Comforter—John 14:16-18; Isa. 51:12.

As a Father Pitieth—Ps. 103:13; Mal. 3:17.

As a Mother Comforteth—Isa. 66:12, 51:12.

Blessed Are They That Mourn—Matt. 5:4; Luke 6:21; Jer. 31:13.

Explained Hereafter—John 13:7; I Cor. 13:12.

God Gave and Hath Taken—Job 1:21, 5:18; Ps. 147:3.

God Our Refuge—Deut. 33:27; Ps. 121:2, 60:11.

His Grace Sufficient—II Cor. 12:9; Deut. 33:25.

I Shall Go to Him—II Sam. 12:23; John 14:2.

It Is Well—II Kings 4:26; Job 2:10; Acts 21:14.

Let Not Your Heart Be Troubled—John 14:1.

Mourning for a Mother—Ps. 35:14; Isa. 66:13.

Mourning for a Son—Jer. 6:26; II Sam. 18:33; Luke 7:12.

Mourning Turned to Joy—Jer. 31:13; Isa. 14:3.

Mutual Comfort—II Cor. 1:4; Isa. 57:18; I Thess. 4:18.

My Sorrow—Lam. 1:12; Jer. 31:12; Rev. 21:4.

Not Comfortless—John 14:18; Isa. 51:12; II Cor. 1:4.

Sorrow Not Without Hope—I Thess. 4:13; Heb. 6:19; Mark 16:10.

Submission—Job 2:10; Isa. 45:9; Ps. 46:10.

Temporal and Eternal—II Cor. 4:18; Gal. 6:8; Heb. 9:15.

The Compassionate Christ—Luke 7:13; Ps. 86:15; John 11:33.

The Hiding of His Hand—John 13:7; I Cor. 13:12; II Cor. 3:18.

The Mother of Sorrows—Luke 2:35; John 19:25-27.

The Seen and the Unseen—II Cor. 4:18; Rom. 8:24; I Pet. 1:8.

The Shadow of Death—Morning—Amos 5:8; Zech. 14:7; Ps. 23.

The Unfailing Friend—Josh. 1:5; Ps. 27:10; Prov. 18:24.

They Comfort Me—Ps. 23:4; II Cor. 1:2-3.

Thy Will Be Done—Matt. 6:10; Acts 21:14.

Useless Weeping—Mark 16:10; John 20:15; I Thess. 4:13.

FRAILTY OF LIFE

But a Step to Death—I. Sam. 20:3; Luke 12:20; Jas. 4:13-15.

Days Numbered—Job 14:5; Ps. 39:4, 90:10-12; Acts 17:31.

Departing—Phil. 1:23; II Cor. 5:8; II Tim. 4:6.

Fear of Death—Heb. 2:15; Rom. 8:15; Matt. 10:28.

No Rest Here—Heb. 4:8; Ps. 55:6; Matt. 11:28.

Oh for the Wings of a Dove!—Ps. 55:6; Isa. 60:8.

Over Jordan—II Sam. 19:36; Josh. 1:11, 4:23.

Sojourners Here—I Chron. 29:15; Ps. 39:12; Heb. 11:9; I Pet. 1:17.

Steps Numbered—Job 14:16, 31:4; Prov. 16:9.

The Weaver's Shuttle—Job 7:6; Isa. 38:12.

Where is Your Hope?—Job 27:14; I Thess. 4:13; Ps. 16:9.

IMMORTALITY

A Crown of Life—Rev. 2:10; I Cor. 9:25.

Alive for Evermore—Rev. 1:18; Ps. 133:3.

Assurance Forever—Isa. 32:17; Acts 17:31.

Blessed Are the Dead—Rev. 14:13; Eccles. 4:2.

Captivity Captive—Ps. 68:18; Eph. 4:8.

Christ's Triumph over Death—Rev. 11:18.

Dead, yet Speaking—Heb. 11:4, 9:16, 17.

Destruction of Death—Hos. 13:14; I Cor. 15:54; Rev. 20:14.

Eternal Life—John 3:16, 10:28, 17:3; I John 5:11.

Ever with the Lord—I Thess. 4:17; John 14:3; I Thess. 5:10.

From Death to Life—I John 3:14; II Cor. 4:12; John 10:10.

I Know That My Redeemer Liveth—Job 19:25; John 11:25.

I Shall Be Satisfied—Ps. 17:15, 36:8, 65:4.

Judge of the Quick and Dead—Acts 10:42; II Tim. 4:1.

Life and Death Ours—I Cor. 3:22; Rom. 8:38.

Life for Evermore—Ps. 133:3; Heb. 7:16.

Life from the Dead—Rom. 11:15; John 12:24; I Cor. 15:53-54.

Light in the Shadow of Death—Job 12:22; Luke 1:79.

Lord of the Living—Rom. 14:9; Matt. 22:32; Heb. 11:19.

No More Death—Rev. 21:4; Heb. 2:14; II Tim. 1:10.

Redeemed from the Grave—Ps. 49:15; Hos. 13:14; I Cor. 15.

Seeking the Living Among the Dead—Luke 24:5; John 20:2-10.

Shall Never See Death—John 8:51-52, 11:26; Heb. 11:5.

The Dead Shall Hear His Voice—John 5:25-29; Acts 17:31.

The God of the Living—Matt. 22:32; Rom. 14:9; Acts 10:36.

The Hope of the Righteous—Prov. 14:32; Num. 23:10.

The Living Hope—(R. V.) I Pet. 1:3-4; Col. 1:5; Heb. 6:11.

The Path of Life—Ps. 16:11; Matt. 7:14; Prov. 15:24.

Victory in Death—Isa. 25:8; Hos. 13:14; I Cor. 15:55-57.

We Shall Not Die—Hab. 1:12; Luke 20:36; John 6:50.

With Christ Living or Dying—Rom. 6:8; II Tim. 2:11.

Works Follow—Rev. 14:13, 20:13; Rom. 14:7.

RESURRECTION

A Mystery Revealed—I Thess. 4:13; I Cor. 15:51.

According to the Scriptures—Luke 24:45-46.

Corruption and Incorruption—I. Cor. 15:42.

He is Risen—Matt. 28:6; Luke 24:6, 34; Rom. 8:29.

I Am the Resurrection—John 11:25, 5:21.

Keystone of the Gospel—I Cor. 15:14-17.

Life from the Dead—I Cor. 15:36; Job 14:7-9.

Paul's Testimony—Acts 23:6; Rom. 1:4; I Cor. 15:8.

Peter's Testimony—Acts 2:24, 32, 4:10; I Pet. 1:3.

Promise to the Fathers—Acts 26:6; Matt. 22:32; Mark 12:27.

Recompense in the Resurrection—Luke 14:14.

Seeking the Living Among the Dead—Luke 24:5; John 12:24.

The Change—I Cor. 15: 51-52; Phil. 3:21.

The Earthly and the Heavenly—I Cor. 15:47-48; Dan. 12:2.

The Last Enemy Destroyed—I Cor. 15:26.

JUDGMENT

According to the Gospel—Rom. 2:16; II Cor. 5:10.

Book of Life—Rev. 20:15; Luke 10:20; Dan. 12:1; Phil. 4:3.

Book of Remembrance—Mal. 3:16-18; Ps. 56:8; Isa. 65:6.

Books Opened—Rev. 20:12; Dan. 7:10, 12:1.

Heart Judgment—I john 2:20-21; Eccles. 3:17; Jer. 11:20; Heb. 8:10.

Inasmuch—Matt. 25:40-45, 10:42; Heb. 6:10.

Jesus the Judge—Matt. 25:31; Acts 17:31; II Cor. 5:10; Ps. 50:1.

Judge of Nations—Gen. 15:4; Ps. 110:6.

Judge of Quick and Dead—II Tim. 4:1; I Pet. 4:5.

Justice and Judgment—Ps. 89:14, 97:2; Jer. 23:5; Prov. 1:24-31.

Mercy and Judgment—Ps. 101:1; Matt. 5:7.

Righteous Rewarded—Matt. 25:34; Rom. 2:10.

Saints Gathered—Ps. 50:5, 6; Deut. 33:3; Mal. 3:16-18.

Secrets Revealed—Eccles. 12:14; Ps. 90:8; Rom. 2:16; I Cor. 4:5.

The Angels—Matt. 13:39, 49, 25:31; Mark 8:38.

The Heavens and the Earth—II Pet. 3:10; Ps. 102:26; Matt. 24:35.

The Judge Cometh—I Chron. 16:33; Ps. 98:9.

The Judgment Throne—Ps. 9:7; II Cor. 5:10; Rev. 20:11.

The Righteous Judge—Gen. 18:25; Ps. 98:9; II Tim. 4:8.

HEAVEN

A Better Country—Heb. 11:16; Phil. 3:20.

Coming to Zion—Isa. 51:11; Jer. 50:5.

Eye Hath Not Seen—I Cor. 2:9; Isa. 64:4.

Face to Face—I Cor. 13:12; Isa. 33:17; Rev. 22:4; I John 3:2.

Incorruptible Inheritance—I Pet. 1:4; Matt. 25:34; Eph. 1:18.

Kingdom of Heaven—Matt. 8:11, 7:21, 5:19, 18:3-4.

Many Mansions—John 14:2; Rev. 14:1-3, 5:11; Ps. 68:17.

New Heaven and New Earth—Rev. 21:1; Isa. 65:17; II Pet. 3:13.

Out of Great Tribulation—Rev. 7:14; Rom. 8:17; Acts 14:22.

White-robed Multitude—Rev. 7:13-15, 19:14.

Whole Family in Heaven—Eph. 3:15; Gen. 12:3; Isa. 8:18.

FOR A CHILD

A Child Called—II Sam. 3:8; Matt. 18:2; Matt. 2:15.

A Child of Prayer—I Sam. 1:27; Luke 1:13; II Kings 4:14-17.

A Little Child Shall Lead Them—Isa. 11:6; Mark 10:15.

All is Well—Mark 7:37; II Kings 4:26; Job 1:21.
Babes Praising God—Matt. 21:15-16; Ps. 8:2.
Can a Mother Forget?—Isa. 49:15; I Sam. 1:28.
Death in Every House—Exod. 12:30; Jer. 9:21.
Desolate—Isa. 49:21; Jer. 10:20, 31:15-17.
Died on Mother's Knees—II Kings 4:18-26.
Disconsolate—Jer. 31:15-17; Isa. 49:21; Jer. 10:20.
First Fruits—Rev. 14:1-5; Zech. 8:5; I Cor. 15:20.
Gathered Lilies—Song of Sol. 6:2; I Sam. 2:33; I Pet. 1:24.
Given to God—Gen. 22:12; I Sam. 1:28; Luke 2:22.
Giving and Taking—Job 1:21; II Kings 4:26.
God's Will Concerning Children—Matt. 18:14; Mark 10:14.
Greatest of All—Matt. 18:1-4; Ps. 131:1-2.
Heaven Full of Children—Zech. 8:5; Matt. 18:10.
I Shall Go to Him—II Sam. 12:23; Matt. 18:2-10.
It is Well—II Kings 4:26; Mark 7:37; Job 1:21.
Lambs in His Arms—Isa. 40:11; Mark 10:16.
Like a Little Child—Matt. 18:3; Mark 10:15.
My Jewels—Mal. 3:17; Mark 10:14; Matt. 18:10.
No More Death—Rev. 21:4; I Cor. 15:26; Isa. 25:8.
Of Such is the Kingdom—Matt. 19:14; Mark 10:14.
Our Angels in Heaven—Matt. 18:10; Rev. 14:1-5.
Refused to Be Comforted—Gen. 37:34-35; Jer. 31:15; Matt. 2:17-18.
Resignation—I Sam. 3:18; Job 1:21; Luke 22:42.
Safe in the Arms of Jesus—Mark 10:16; Isa. 40:11.
Suffer Them to Come—Matt. 19:14; Mark 10:14.
The Child is Not—Gen. 37:30; Jer. 10:20.
The Ministry of Childhood—Isa. 11:6; Matt. 18:4.

The Widow's Child—I Kings 17:17; Luke 7:12.

They Shall Come Again—Jer. 31:16; I Thess. 4:14; II Sam. 12:33.

Thou Shalt Know Hereafter—John 13:7; Ps. 97:2; II Kings 4:26.

Vision of God's Face—Matt. 18:10; Rev. 22:4.

Voice out of the Cloud—Matt. 17:5; Ps. 97:2.

Weeping at Night, Joy in Morning—Ps. 30:5; Amos 5:8; Rev. 22:5.

What Manner of Child?—Luke 1:66, 2:19; Heb. 11:23.

Where the Treasure Is—Matt. 6:21, 18:10, 19:14.

Without Fault—Rev. 14:5; Matt. 18:10, 19:14; Mark 10:14.

FOR A YOUNG PERSON

Behold, the Bridegroom Cometh—Matt. 25:6, 13; Amos 4:12.

Death of a Daughter—Mark 5:35; Judg. 11:40.

Death of a Son—II Sam. 18:33; Luke 7:12.

Death of a Young Man—Jer. 9:21, 48:17; Isa. 40:30.

God's Covenant with Youth—Ezek. 16:60; Matt. 19:20.

Honorable Youth—I Tim. 4:12; Acts 26:4; Matt. 19:20; Dan. 1:8.

Rejoice in Youth—Eccles. 11:9, 12:1; Ps. 90:14.

Remember Thy Creator—Eccles. 12:1; Ps. 90:14.

Seek Him—Amos 5:8; Isa. 55:6; Ps. 27:8.

Strength and Beauty—I Kings 7:22; Prov. 20:29.

Thy Son Liveth—I Kings 17:23; Heb. 11:35; Luke 7:15.

FOR A PERSON IN MIDDLE LIFE

A Soldier's Death—II Tim. 4:7-8; Josh. 23:14.
Business Interrupted—Jas. 4:13-14; Luke 12:20.
Death of a Brother—II Sam. 1:26; John 11:23.
Death of a Deacon—Acts 6:5, 7:54-60.
Death of a Good Man—Acts 7:59-60; Prov. 12:2.
Death of a Good Woman—Acts 9:36-39.
Death of a Husband—Joel 1:8; Song of Sol. 3:2.
Death of a Minister—Acts 20:24; II Tim. 4:5.
Death of a Sister—Num. 20:1; Acts 9:36-39.
Death of a Wife—Gen. 48:7; Prov. 31:10-31.
In the Midst of Life—Ps. 102-24; Jer. 15:9; Isa. 38:10.
Life's Silver Cord—Eccles. 12:6, 4:12; Jer. 10:20.
To Die is Gain—Phil. 1:21; II Cor. 5:8; II Tim. 4:6.

FOR AN AGED PERSON

A Good Fight—II Tim. 4:7; Phil. 3:14; Heb. 12:1.
A Good Old Age—Gen. 15:15, 25:8; Isa. 46:4.
Abiding or Departing—Phil. 1:23-24; II Cor. 5:8.
As Gold Tried—Job 23:10; Zech. 13:9; Prov. 17:3.
At Rest—Job 3:17; II Tim. 1:7; Rev. 14:13.
Blessed Dead—Rev. 14:13; Eccles. 4:2; Rev. 20:6.
Chariot of the Lord—II Kings 2:11; Gen. 5:24.
Crown of Glory—Prov. 16:31, 20:29; II Tim. 4:8.
Days Numbered—Job 14:5; Ps. 90:10, 12, 39:4.
Death Knell of All—Gen. 5:27; Eccles. 3:20; Heb.
    9:27.
Death of a Father—Gen. 25:8; II Kings 2:12.
Death of a Mother—Ps. 35:14; Prov. 31:1; Isa. 66:13.

Death of God's Saints—Ps. 116:15, 34:22; Num. 23:10.

Death of the Righteous—Num. 23:10; Ps. 37:37, 116:15.

Desire Accomplished—Luke 2:29-30; Gen. 46:30.

Fear of Death Removed—Heb. 2:14-15; Ps. 23:4.

Gathered Home—Gen. 49:33; Eccles. 12:5; John 14:2.

Glad Homecoming—Isa. 51:11, 35:10; Rev. 21:25.

God Took Him—Gen. 5:24; II Kings 2:11; Heb. 11:5.

Guide Unto Death—Ps. 48:14, 23:4; Ps. 73:24.

Hope in Death—Prov. 14:32; Gen. 46:30; Phil. 1:23.

Inheritance of a Good Man—Prov. 13:22, 22:1.

Into the Morning—Amos 5:8; Ps. 30:5; Isa. 58:8.

Light Affliction, Exceeding Glory—II Cor. 4:17.

Light at Evening Time—Zech. 14:7; Prov. 4:18; Isa. 58:8.

My Change—Job 14:14; Phil. 3:21; I Cor. 15:51; II Cor. 3:18.

Over Jordan—II Sam. 19:36; Jer. 12:5; Josh. 1:11.

Quiet Resting Places—Isa. 32:18; Ps. 23:2; Rev. 14:13.

Quietness and Assurance—Isa. 32:17; Job 3:17.

Ripe for Harvest—Job 5:26; Prov. 16:31; Isa. 46:4.

The End of All—Eccles. 7:2, 3:20; Heb. 9:27; Ps. 89:48.

The Fountain of Life—Ps. 36:9; Jer. 2:13; John 4:14.

The King in His Beauty—Isa. 33:17; Matt. 5:8; Rev. 22:4.

Valley of the Shadow—Ps. 23:4, 44:19; Job 10:21-22.

Victory over Death—I Cor. 15:54; Isa. 25:8; Rev. 20:14.

Waiting for Death—Job 14:14; Ps. 27:14; II Tim. 4:6-7.

Work Ended—Eccles. 9:10; Job 17:11; John 9:4, 17:4.

Works Follow Them—Rev. 14:13; Heb. 6:10; Rev. 22:12.

INDEX OF SCRIPTURE READINGS

INDEX OF PRAYERS

215

INDEX OF HYMNS AND POEMS

INDEX OF AUTHORS

INDEX BY CLASSIFICATIONS

223